SIMPLE INVESTOR GUIDE

JOHN SINGH

Publisher Information

First published 2023

ISBN 978-0-6457473-0-0

Disclaimer

The information provided in this book is shared only for educational purposes. This information does not constitute as financial advice and should not be solely relied upon as each individual's situation is different and subject to interpretation. The author believes that the opinions and figures provided in this book, and references to other sources or websites, are reliable, however, no guarantees are made about their accuracy. The author does not accept any responsibility or liability as a result of any actions or losses incurred from acting on the content provided in this book. All readers must do their research and are responsible for their decisions.

Acknowledgements

Writing this book has been an interesting journey, although it took a bit longer than I anticipated to complete.

My passion for writing the book would not have been possible without my family's support.

I wish to acknowledge and give thanks to my wife, Amreeta, for her support and encouragement in writing this book, and to my son, Jaasiel, for undertaking the preliminary edit.

A very special thanks to my daughter, Aminta, for her enormous contribution to the layout, design, final edit, and formatting of this book.

About the Author

John Singh is a real estate and share market investor. He has been an accountant for large organisations and has extensive expertise in revenue and investment. He has had many years of hands-on experience in real estate, investment, and treasury management, including bonds and interest rates.

His successful career and fruitful investment decisions have led him to share his knowledge and experiences in this book to make a positive impact on others' lives.

CONTENTS

INTRODUCTION

One needs to determine the type of investment that will suit an individual, taking into account the objectives of that person and how it will contribute to funding your future retirement or serve in lieu of replacing your current employment income.

There are many modes of investment but, in this book, I will focus on property and shares. While there is always an element of risk in investment, it is important to assess and minimise risk to determine the best approach and fit for your financial capacity.

The three types of investment that I focus on are:

- Purchasing a Home (to live in)
- Purchasing an Investment Property
- Share Trading

Each of the above requires various knowledge and financial capacity to invest. Some of you may have some expertise in these fields but there are various professionals who can advise you on these investment strategies by charging fees.

At the end of the day, you need to be in control of all transactions and be informed enough to make reasonable judgements and decisions about your investments.

PART 1 - PURCHASING PROPERTIES

1. PURCHASING SUMMARY

Buying an investment property is a little bit different from buying your own home where you yourself intend to live. Buying a home to live in will entail many aspects where you will need to make decisions that affect your family and social lifestyle. You will need to assess what facilities are available nearby, the commuting distance, the status or condition of the property, and whether you need funds to upgrade the property and to have a buffer for any unexpected future repairs.

There are also emotional factors in buying a home to live in. You will need to draw up a checklist of what you are really looking for, what your budget is, and in what price range you are looking to buy. These factors will vary widely between each potential home buyer.

A common factor when seeking a home loan is your capacity to borrow. You need to research your options by communicating with banks and assessing whether your borrowing capacity fits the bank's lending criteria. Once you have met the lending criteria for a specific bank, you may be granted a conditional or unconditional pre-approved loan.

There are some important factors to take into consideration before signing the final loan approval documents to avoid future fees that may be incurred if changes are made after the initial loan approval.

In addition to the interest rate offered, there will be other fundamental factors to determine whether you are being offered a good deal from the bank. These factors may influence your borrowing decision:

- Principal and interest loan repayment
- Interest-only loan repayment
- Fixed or variable loan
- Partially fixed & variable loans
- Special interest rate discounts

- Offering a credit card attached to the home loan with no yearly fees
- How much the bank is willing to offer the loan without mortgage insurance
- Special deals, such as cashback
- Loan backed by security against other property
- Home loan offset account
- Re-draw facility

The borrowing processes of banks and financial institutions vary, with the most important difference being the quality of customer service that you are offered. It is always advisable to shop around for the best deal and service.

Purchasing your first home may be challenging and some of you may be entering uncharted territory. It is key to remember that nothing is impossible and that there is a vast amount of information, data and research available now as compared to only 10-20 years ago.

Before going home hunting, every potential buyer needs to assess their financial capacity. The most obvious way to proceed is to obtain a pre-approved loan. Pre-approved loans can be conditional or unconditional.

Apart from obtaining a loan, it is also important to consider the upfront costs, or outflow, involved in buying a home.

Analysing the upfront costs will guide you on the price range of the house you are looking for however obtaining a loan will also be subject to the additional outflow:

- How much deposit is required by the bank (10% or 20%)?
- Do you qualify for stamp duty exemption?
- What is the estimated legal cost?
- What type of home are you buying (i.e., existing, new, single dwelling, duplex, etc)?

There are a few categories of property to consider when purchasing a property:

1) Purchasing an existing home
2) Purchasing a new home as a house and land package
3) Purchasing land and then building a house
4) Purchasing a unit, townhouse or villa

It is advisable when obtaining a pre-approved loan to inform the bank about what you intend to buy (i.e., a house, unit or a construction loan to buy the land and then build a house) so that the loan can be tailored accordingly if you need to draw down funds during a construction phase.

Each of the above purchases will require various searches before entering into a contract of sale, including searches arranged through your solicitor.

A considerable amount of thought needs to go into buying a property. As you will be outlaying a substantial amount of money, do not rush to buy a property. First, monitor the property market by evaluating similar properties that have been listed for sale or sold. This will give you a fair idea of the price range and condition of the property. The objective is to ensure that you are not paying too much for a property with an inflated price as listed on the market.

2. TYPES OF PROPERTY PURCHASES

Purchasing an Established Home

Existing or established homes are listed on the market by real estate agents as a private treaty sale or by auction. Properties are open for inspection until an offer has been received or a contract signed and exchanged.

Before a property inspection, you must do your own research for the properties you intend to view:

- Location
- Size of the home and the land
- The current state of the property
- Neighbourhood
- Transportation
- Easy access to roads and motorways
- Schools
- Shopping complex
- Community facilities
- Price range – compare with similar properties on the market or recently sold

Property Inspection

Once you have identified which properties to inspect, the following must be assessed before you make an offer:

- Ensure you have looked at recent sales within the area with similar features.
- Are you buying in a rising market or a slowing economy?
- What is the current condition of the property, such as the age of the property and any future repairs or replacements that will be required. As this is not a brand-new home, you must allow some financial buffer for unexpected repairs.
- Some house listings are initially overpriced. On some occasions the price is reduced after some time. This will give a good indication that the original listed price was inflated.
- How long has the property been on the market? The longer the duration, the greater the potential for a price reduction.
- Who is residing on the property? Is it the owner or is it currently being leased? If it is currently leased, you must investigate

when the lease expires. If the tenant does not have a fixed term lease, what is their current arrangement with the landlord?

- Obtain a copy of the contract of sale and read it thoroughly, even though your solicitor will go through it with you once you sign the contract and pay a 0.25% holding deposit.
- With your solicitor and the real estate agent, discuss getting vacant possession of the property upon settlement to avoid incurring additional costs after settlement if the tenant is still residing at the property.
- Have the finance (loan) pre-approved.

Making an Offer

Once you have assessed all the relevant conditions, you can make a reasonable offer. In most cases the offer should be less than the listed price or asking price. Your offer could be accepted or rejected and renegotiated.

If an offer is accepted, you have succeeded. If rejected, you can propose to negotiate. This is where you must be careful.

The dollar value will count here as the vendor and agent are desperate to sell and may seek to persuade you into the trap of increasing your offer.

At the end of the day, this is your decision. Remember this is not the only property in the market, there are other properties that you could look at.

Golden rule is to never rush into buying a home. Eventually, you will get the right home you want at a reasonable price.

Offer Accepted

On the other hand, if the offer is accepted, in most cases the following process will take place:

- You, as the buyer, will need to sign the contract of sale in the presence of the real estate agent and pay a holding deposit of

0.25% of the contract price. You will be given a cooling off period of 5-10 days for your solicitor to conduct various searches.

- The buyer's solicitor will receive the contract from the selling agent.
- Your solicitor will make an appointment with you to go through the contract and will conduct various searches.
- If the property is occupied by a tenant, you should obtain written assurance that upon the settlement date you will need vacant possession of the property if you intend to live in the property immediately or otherwise on a specified agreed upon date.
- Where applicable, ensure an asbestos inspection is conducted by a qualified inspector.
- You can pull out of the contract within the cooling off period if there are any problems with the searches or the property, however, you will forfeit the holding deposit of 0.25%.
- If no issues are found in all the conducted searches and you and your solicitor are

satisfied, then you will proceed with the contract and pay a 10% deposit of the contract price to the selling agent. This deposit can be paid by a bank cheque, bank guarantee or EFT as well.

- Review any special conditions in the contract with your solicitor.

Purchasing House and Land Package

Newly built homes are usually in new suburbs or in a new land release area. These homes have a fixed price cost which may have most inclusions similar to what you expect in buying an established home. As for an established home, you must assess several key facilities before you proceed with a decision to purchase a house and land package:

- Research the developer and the builder
- Transportation
- Easy access to roads and motorways
- Schools

- Shopping complex
- Community facilities

These are some of the key factors that should be seriously considered when settling for a house and land package. These are also most common when buying any other brand-new property on the market.

Due diligence is a *must* in this situation to avoid future pitfalls and the risk of losing thousands of dollars if the property is not structurally sound. Ensure the builder is reputable.

Some developers have certain guidelines for builders to adhere to when dwellings are constructed. Ensure the builder has taken the cost factor into account so you are not up for additional costs later. (e.g., a developer may require a specific design, facade or fencing type).

There are generally two types of house and land packages:

- Homes that are already built and you could move in within months of purchase. These are already built homes sold as complete house and land packages. In this instance, you can inspect the brand-new home and decide if you wish to settle for it. So, ultimately you get what you see and it's similar to buying an existing home, except the home is brand-new.

- Project Home Builders will build a home as per their display home specifications. In this instance, the parcel of land is available and the home will be built once you sign the contract. This would take approximately 6-12 months depending on the builder, house specifications and weather conditions. Here, you have a choice of design, but you also need to determine what inclusions are in the contract (e.g., fencing, landscaping, driveway and site costs).

Purchasing Land to Build a House

Purchasing land and then building a house calls for a different perspective and some knowledge about buying land.

In most cases land is available in the new release area as with a house and land package deal. The difference is that the buyer purchases the land first and then later builds a house according to their choice and affordability. It may be built immediately or at a later time.

Buying Land

Deciding to buy land will depend on the location, current infrastructure and planned future developments. You would also look for:

- The size of land required. At this stage you should have a fair idea about what sort of house you intend to build and ensure the prospective house will fit on the land.

- It will cost you more to build if a lot of modifications are needed to fit the house on the land.
- Easement – if there is any encumbrance that is part of the land. Your solicitor should be able to give you advice on this matter.
- Any restrictions by the developer in the construction of the house. Sometimes the developer may insert certain restrictions regarding the type of fencing, facade, driveways, etc.
- The land should be registered, if it is not registered, your plans to build the house may be delayed.
- Transportation.
- Easy access to roads and motorways.
- Schools.
- Shopping complex.
- Community facilities.

Once the land has been purchased and settled, you can then get on with planning and obtaining quotes to start construction. The longer you take to proceed with the construction, the longer you will be paying interest on the mortgage of the land unless you have purchased the land for cash.

Here you have two options, either to build through a project home company or build it yourself by obtaining an owner-builder's permit.

Project Homes - For most people this may be the most viable option. Project home builders have the expertise to guide you on what your options are and will give an approximate cost of the house you choose.

Obtaining a fixed cost quote should be the priority. Project home companies that do not give you fixed cost quote can cost you additional thousands of dollars when they commence work on the land.

Some costs could be piering, soil testing, surveying and excavation costs. If these costs are variable and not fixed then during the construction you will have to pay additional costs.

Building as an Owner Builder – This is most suitable for those who have a fair idea of the building industry. First, you must have an Owner Builder's Licence before you proceed with any work. You need to do the costing whether it's cheaper to proceed as an owner builder or to go through a project home company.

Key points to operate as an owner builder.

1. Have a relevant insurance cover during the period of construction.
2. Ensure workplace safety is maintained at all times for all workers and anyone visiting the property at any given point in time.
3. The house plan must be approved by the appropriate authorities.
4. Works are subcontracted to licensed trades people.
5. Seek quotes from builders and tradies for each stage of work.
6. Ensure inspections are carried out at required stages as prescribed by the council or appropriated approving body.

7. Deal with contractors who hold appropriate licences which can be verified by the Department of Fair-Trading NSW or the relevant body in your state.
8. Must have the time to inspect each stage of construction and ensure it is progressing so that construction is not put on hold and delayed.

Purchasing a Unit/Townhouse/Villa/ Duplex

Purchasing a unit, townhouse, villa or duplex is different from buying a house. There are pros and cons to be considered before contemplating to purchase.

Purchasing a Unit/Apartment

When purchasing a unit, the location will be an important factor in deciding where to live and also determining supply and demand within the suburb.

Units and apartments are governed by the strata laws and all owners are bound by strata policy and procedures. These are some information which all prospective buyers should be aware of when they consider buying a unit or apartment:

- Location - where you wish to buy. In most cases buyers would like to stay within the vicinity of public transport, shopping complex, school and preferably hospitals and universities.
- Find out who is the Strata Manager.
- Always obtain a strata report before entering into a contract. The strata report will give you important information about the whole complex including its sinking fund, strata levy per quarter or any additional levies that are being imposed. Also consider whether there is any major future maintenance to be undertaken.
- Parking facilities within the complex with either a lock-up garage or an undercover car space.
- The number of units and apartments in the complex.

- Does it have an internal laundry and balcony?
- The upkeep and presentation of the overall complex.

Purchasing a Villa

A villa is a single home dwelling with its own courtyard within a complex that includes several similar dwellings.

Villas mostly consist of two or three bedrooms with garage and is under strata, so strata fees are applicable.

Purchasing a Townhouse

A townhouse may be multi-floored and may be attached or free-standing within a complex that includes a number of similar homes.

Townhouses often include a courtyard and a garage or car space and may have a separate entrance. These are mostly governed by strata laws.

Purchasing a Duplex

A duplex is a building that comprises of two homes with a common central wall. Duplexes can be a single storey or a double storey.

The homes could be on one land title or have a separate title for each home. If each home is on separate title, it can be sold separately.

Owner-Builder

The most important aspect to decide before proceeding to be an owner-builder is to determine if this is for you. Do you have the know-how and are you up to it? What is the motivating factor and the reason for wanting to be an owner-builder?

This should be strategically thought about, not with an emotional thought. Once you have decided to go with the owner builder concept, there are many processes to follow with care.

First, obtain an owner-builder permit. The prospective owner-builder will need to have relevant skills and capacity to build their own house and also be able to supervise the construction work.

There are some restrictions that an owner-builder permit cannot be issued for:

- Renovations or alterations to the apartment, unit or townhouse.
- A property that is not for a residential purpose but for other use.
- All trade work that requires a licence such as plumbing or electrical work, should be carried out by personnel with a relevant licence.
- To be an owner-builder you should be aware of certain aspects of an owner builder's responsibility. You will be liable and will take all responsibility when you take on this task.
- Note, an owner-builder permit is not a builder's licence.

Advantages of being an Owner-Builder

- Choice of design.
- Allows flexibility to make amendments to your choice without excessive cost as compared to project home companies.
- Gives you an utter most control of the entire construction process.
- Easier to make changes to your budget in case of financial crisis or unexpected situations.
- Building project can be delayed due to unforeseen circumstances.

Key points to be an Owner-Builder.

- You should be over 18 years of age.
- You should be the owner of the land on which the construction will be done or the owner of the home where the additions will be made.
- Ensure you have an owner-builder permit and the relevant council's construction permit approval before you commence construction.

- It is always advisable that you obtain or seek advice from your Local Council, Department of Fair Trading, or similar authorising body in your state regarding the owner-builder conditions.
- Ensure you have relevant insurances that are required to cover yourself for any accidents or mishaps on the construction site. Some relevant insurances include:
  1. Workers' compensation insurance
  2. Contract works insurance
  3. Public liability insurance
  4. Home builders' insurance
  5. Sub-contracting work: You may subcontract works as you see fit and ensure sub-contractors are licenced trade personnel.

How to commence the owner builder process

- *Seek assistance from an Architect* – they will assist you to make decisions on what's required regarding the final plans and application approvals.

- *Complete the Owner Builder's Course* – this course is available online through various organisations and you will need to check the conditions and requirements within your state. Once you have completed the Owner Builder Course, you can submit your application to Service NSW or the relevant organisation in your state.

- *Prepare to submit the application to the council* – you should also contact your local council in your state for clarity.

- *Ensure all Insurances are in place* – refer to previous pages on the various types of insurance.

- *Commence Work* – once all applications have been granted, including council approval, you can then start construction.

You will be responsible for all aspects of the building work performed as an owner-builder such as:

- Ensure you oversee the project unless you have appointed a project manager.
- Ensure appropriate inspections are conducted at regular intervals by the appropriate governing body. E.g., before laying the slab, the site should be inspected.
- Your responsibility towards workers' safety is paramount during the tenure of the building project.
- Ensure only licenced contractors are used for specific works such as plumbing and electrical, and that all contractors are adequately insured.
- Ensure any quotes received for contractual work are in writing to avoid future disputes.
- Contractors' licences can be verified with Service NSW or the relevant governing body in your state. This is an important check which will indicate if the contractor's licence is valid and if there are any past or pending disputes lodged against the contractor.

3. SEEKING A LOAN

Banks and Finance Brokers

Banks will be a major contributor to the property purchase. The loan manager is one of the most important people during the life of a loan. The loan manager will be able to assist in changing the loan structure, if needed, or in applying for an additional loan in the future. So, it's not only the bank that is critical, but it is also getting a good loans manager who can tailor your loan requirements.

Once you have selected a bank, you will proceed with the loan. Based on your circumstances, you will determine your preferred loan structure.

Another option is to obtain a loan from another type of financial institution through a mortgage broker, but one must carefully understand what are the benefits and conditions of this approach.

Including additional people on an application will improve your prospects of obtaining a loan. This practice can be beneficial for younger people who are trying to get into the market in the current climate. By including parents, relatives, or other trusted people in the application, you will have greater prospects of obtaining a loan as it is backed by several people with a higher income stream.

If you are purchasing an investment property, this would play a vital role in the event where you wish to sell the property in the near future. When you sell an investment property, you are liable to pay capital gains tax. So, if there is more than one owner, the capital gains cost will be shared amongst all owners of the property.

Finance brokers act as an agent to secure the loan for you. If you intend to use a finance broker to seek a home loan, they will require you to provide various details to assess your financial capacity to borrow. Finance brokers will also recommend which loan package is better for you and from which financial institutions you may borrow.

Brokers work with various lenders and their ultimate objective should be to get you the best deal but bear in mind that brokers are paid on commission by the lenders for the product they sell to you on the lender's behalf.

For clarity, you must verify the following issues with a broker before you proceed with them:

- Are they going to charge you fees?
- How many lenders do they deal with and who are they?
- The commission they receive may vary between lenders. You must ensure that you get the best home loan package. Some brokers may be paid a higher commission for recommending specific types of loan which may not be in your best interest.

Types of Home Loan Products

There are various types of loans, including:

- Principal and interest repayments
- Interest repayments only
- Line of credit
- Variable rate

- Fixed rate
- Split loan - with both features, partial variable and partial fixed interest rate
- Offset account
- Redraw facility

Principal and Interest Repayments

Most buyers take this option. Any payment towards the home loan reduces your principal which is the original amount of the loan. Additional payments reduce the term of the loan quickly. The important aspect of this loan is that you are also building equity for any future property investments or if you wish to use equity for other purposes.

Example: Your home loan is $500,000. For the last two years you have been paying principal and interest and your loan has been reduced to $460,000, thus you have an estimated equity of $40,000.

Interest Repayments Only

Interest repayments will only cover the interest portion of your loan. This type of loan favours property investors as it is the most beneficial for tax advantages.

Interest-only repayments are for a specified number of years or as agreed with the bank. At the conclusion of the interest-only period, the loan will revert to interest and principal, unless you apply for a further interest-only payment option.

In this option, your principal (original loan amount) will remain the same and you will have less equity available than if you were to pay principal plus interest. For the total duration of the loan period, you would pay more interest when compared to the interest and principal payment option.

Line of Credit

This is a secured overdraft against your house as a security and will enable the home-owner to use funds for any purpose.

You can draw funds as the need arises. You will only pay interest on the amount you withdraw and not on the total line of credit. One of the major advantages of a line of credit is that the funds are readily available and ready to use at anytime and you do not have to seek approval or take another loan. However, interest on this type of loan is normally higher than a home loan or an investment loan.

Example: If your line of credit is $250,000 and you have used $50,000, you will only be charged interest on $50,000.

Home Loan Redraw Facility

Any additional repayments you have made on your home loan could be redrawn for any purpose during the term of the loan.

A redraw facility offers tax advantages for investment properties. If funds are held in a savings account, any interest earned is taxable but whereas savings held in the home loan account are not taxed and will save on the monthly interest paid on the home loan.

Example: You have a home loan of $300,000 with an interest rate payable of 3% per annum and also have $30,000 in a savings account with an interest rate receivable of 1%.

The interest earned on $30,000 savings would be $300.00 per annum and will be taxed along with your annual income. If the $30K is deposited into the home loan account, you would be saving around $75.00 a month on interest payments for your home loan.

Variable Rate Home Loan

When you take out a loan, the bank will allocate a variable home loan rate to your mortgage. This rate can fluctuate if the Reserve Bank increases or decreases the cash rate.

The change in interest rate on mortgages is dependent on the banks passing the reduction or increase onto their loan customers. Suppose the interest rates goes down by 0.25% as announced by the Reserve Bank, the banks may reduce the interest on mortgage by 0.15% only.

The variable rate home loan is a better option during the cycle or period when interest rates are falling. With a variable home loan rate, it offers an offset facility and also allows you to make additional payments.

Fixed Rate

Fixed interest rate gives you peace of mind on what your monthly/fortnightly or weekly payment will be since the interest rate is fixed. The fixed rate will only be for a specific period of time which may be from 1 – 5 years approximately.

After the fixed period comes to an end, the interest rate will revert to a variable rate unless you negotiate another fixed term with a different fixed rate.

The important aspect to note about a fixed home loan rate is that you will need to pay a penalty if you break the fixed rate period.

Split Loans - with partial variable and fixed interest rate

This loan may also suit quite a few mortgage holders. Here, you can choose to have part of the loan at a variable rate and part of the loan at a fixed rate.

Example: You have a loan of $500,000. You can opt to have $260,000 under a variable rate and $240,000 on a fixed rate. This is mostly based on a mixed market situation where you are not sure of the economic climate that the interest rate may increase or fall in the near future.

Offset Account

This is applicable if you have a home loan and also a savings account. This is a great feature that allows you to pay less interest on the mortgage each month and also helps you to avoid paying tax on the interest that you would have received from the savings.

Example: Your current loan outstanding is $470,000 and you have a savings account balance of $50,000. Before calculating the interest for the month, the banks will offset the $50,000 from $470,000 and the interest will be calculated on $420,000.

Suppose the current home loan interest rate is 2.8% and the interest rate derived from the savings account is around 0.35%. So, the saving on interest payment is $102.00 per month which equates to $1,225.00 per annum.

Your funds generally work better in an offset account in comparison to a normal savings account. The interest you receive from the savings account is mostly lower than what you would pay for your mortgage.

Table 1 – Interest saving calculation

Current Loan	$470,000
Interest Rate	2.80%
Interest - Month	$1,097
Loan linked to offset account	
Current Loan	$470,000
Less Savings in offset A/C	$50,000
Total	$420,000
Interest – Month (2.80%)	$980
Savings on Interest	$117
Interest earned on savings account not linked	
Savings	$50,000
Current interest rate on savings a/c	0.35%
Interest earned per month	$15

So, you can see the three steps of calculation. If having an offset, you are in a better position by saving $102 per month ($117 less $15).

Mortgage

There are three modes of mortgage repayments.

- Weekly repayments
- Fortnightly repayments
- Monthly repayments

Weekly or fortnightly payments are a better option for mortgage repayments as you will save a significant amount of money. When paying in monthly instalments you will make 12 payments a year. When paying fortnightly you would make 26 payments and not 24 payments. As interest is calculated daily and charged to the loan on a monthly basis, making an additional payment will reduce the life of the loan.

How to pay off your mortgage before the schedule term?

In most cases, the duration of the mortgage is a 30 year term but it could be paid off earlier if you are vigilant in monitoring the loan with some of the following actions taken:

Making additional payments: Making additional payments on an ad hoc basis or increasing fortnightly payments will reduce the life term of your loan.

Refinancing loans: You may be paying a higher interest rate so you should shop around with other banks to negotiate a better rate or refinance the mortgage for a better deal.

Offset accounts: Use of an offset account is a great feature that allows you to pay less interest on the mortgage.

Interest rate fall: When there is an interest rate reduction, the banks will reduce your fortnightly or monthly repayment but if you continue to pay the original amount instead of the reduction, this will reduce the term of the loan.

Avoid interest only payment: Avoid the interest-only payment feature of the loan, as your principal mortgage amount will never be reduced.

How to purchase property without a deposit

If you are not a first home buyer and have an existing home, your prospect of buying your next property may be a bit easier, depending on the equity you have built on the current property. The new loan you are seeking could be secured against the existing property.

You can also buy a home with no deposit by having a close relative as a guarantor to get your foot into the housing market.

Lenders Mortgage Insurance (LMI)

If you do not have the required deposit of 20% of the property value, the banks may suggest you acquire a lenders' mortgage insurance.

Lenders Mortgage Insurance (LMI) is a one-off fee that banks and other finance lenders charge borrowers when their housing deposit is less than 20% of their property's purchase price.

When a borrower defaults on payment and the bank intends to recover the amount lent, the LMI will come into play:

1. The current outstanding home loan is $700,000 and the lender intends to sell the property to recover this amount.
2. The lender manages to sell the property for $610,000 and the shortfall is $90,000.
3. The lender will seek to recover $90,000 from the LMI provider.
4. The provider in return will seek to recover the amount of $90,000 from the borrower.
5. The most important aspect to understand about LMI is that it is to protect the lender (bank or financial institution) and not the borrower. Without this insurance, the bank would not usually lend to a borrower without the required 20% deposit.

Lending Managers

When dealing with banks or financial institutions, it is important to have a good lending manager. This makes a huge difference when processing loan applications, restructuring the loan, and obtaining further loans for future investments.

Having a good lending manager who can meet your needs by communicating by email or phone can prevent much stress and save the borrower a lot of time that would normally be spent ringing call centres in banks or financial institutions.

It is important to review your dealings with the bank or broker to ensure you are getting a good deal. Something to note is that it is not likely to be worth refinancing for petty interest rate benefits if you have good relations with the current lending manager.

Cross-Collateralisation

Cross-collateralisation occurs when more than one property is used as security for a loan.

Example: You have a property worth $1,000,000 with a current mortgage of $200,000 and you wish to buy another property worth $500,000. The equity in the current property is $800,000 ($1,000,000 less $200,000). In this instance you can avoid paying the required deposit and fees by obtaining a loan with the same lender with cross-collateralisation. Here, the total of the new loan will be secured against your existing property. In other words, two of the loans ($200,000 & $500,000) are secured against the first property.

This approach may allow you to continue to purchase several properties, as long as you meet the valuation and lending criteria of the lending institution.

There is also a downside to cross-collateralisation as each property is not secured separately. If you wish to sell one of your properties which in this case may be the property that is being secured to obtain the second loan then the loan contract and security term would change. You may also be required to provide a current valuation of the remaining properties. If there is a drop in value with the revaluation, the lending institution could take partial proceeds from the sale of the property to satisfy the new lending and security arrangement.

Try to keep each property secured separately to avoid the proceeds from the sale of the property being offset against other loans of this arrangement.

4. PURCHASING PROCESS

I have touched on a few points about buying a property in earlier chapters. Here, I will elaborate on what to look for when buying a property and how to research and assess a property before making an offer. There are three people involved in this phase:

- Real Estate Agent
- Vendor (seller)
- Buyer (you)

Real Estate Agent

The property is listed by the agent who is the person you are in contact with when arranging for an inspection and getting more details on the property.

Vendor

The vendor does not normally get directly involved with the buyer as the agent will act as a representative on their behalf.

Buyer

You, as the buyer, will need to be savvy when purchasing a property. For example, when attending a property inspection do not go empty handed. It is important to do some research and investigate if the listed price is reasonable by looking at similar properties within the area that are being recently listed or sold. This can be done by searching websites where properties are listed.

By comparing past property sales in the near vicinity with similar features you may be amazed with your comparison. Remember, this is only the initial stage prior to a physical inspection where you are yet to see the condition of the property.

When viewing a property, you must be aware of certain descriptive features that are shown and NOT shown on the advertised listings that may ring alarm bells in your mind as a buyer:

- The listed property does not display the shower, bath or toilet. This may indicate that they are in poor or unusable condition.
- The property price is not listed and may state “contact the agent”. If you choose to contact the agent, they may ask you questions such as “how much can you afford” or “how much is your loan being approved for”. Never disclose this information until you have inspected the property and are ready to make an offer.
- The property listing does not provide a location or address. Ask yourself, why would the agent not provide the property location? All buyers would want to know the location of the property. This may be

hidden from the listing due to a poor location.

- The property is advertised with a listed price range such as $800,000 - $850,000. How many buyers will offer $830,000 or above $800,000? With my experience and discussion with agents, the range attracts various bids causing buyers to compete with the price range. An agent's argument is that they will expect three or four offers, so there will be more competition which allows vendors to have the upper hand to accept the offer of the highest bidder. On the other hand, some agents are totally against this approach and have the view that the property should only have one fixed price listed (e.g., $830,000).
- The listing states to *make an offer*. The vendor and agent are putting the buyer in a peculiar situation. There is nothing wrong with doing this, but we all know what the trap is. If the offer is low, the vendor will not accept it but if the offer is high, it will be accepted. You do not know how much the vendor is looking for, the

agent and the vendor are at an upper hand as you may offer more than their expectation.

Example – Property Inspection

A property had been listed but had no pictures displayed of its interior such as the kitchen, toilet, bathroom and bedroom. During the inspection it was identified that the property had ceiling lights hanging down out of the ceiling. There was no kitchen, bath, shower, toilet or flooring and the asking price was ridiculous. There were materials available for the buyer to use to complete the kitchen, bath, toilet, flooring and other missing features.

Always remember to review similar properties online within the same price range and with similar features so you have a fair guide to price. Ensure the website displays all features of the property.

Once you have seen the property online and assessed your buying capacity, only then will you be ready to contact the agent to inspect the property.

As a buyer these are some of the most common features you will look for:

Units/Apartments/Townhouses/Villa/ Duplex

- Size of the space including bedrooms.
- Condition of the toilet and bathroom.
- Condition of the kitchen.
- Condition of the floor.
- Air-conditioning.
- Does it have built-ins?
- Does it have an internal laundry?
- Does it have a balcony?
- Does it need painting?
- What are the other facilities e.g., pool, lifts, etc?
- Parking facilities (car space or lock-up garage).
- Nearby transportation, schools and shopping facilities.
- Read the strata minutes if available.
- What are the strata fees and are there any additional levies in place?
- If a tenant is currently occupying the unit and you are buying to live in it, check with the agent when the lease will expire or

when it will be available for vacant possession.

- If you are buying as an investment, check the current rental market. The current tenant could be paying high rent as they may have been living in the property for a number of years. You should consider that if the property falls vacant then you may get a new tenant at a reduced rental rate.

House

- Number of bedrooms.
- Condition of the toilet and bathrooms.
- Condition of the kitchen.
- Are there easements on the property?
- Are there any extensions made to the original property? This should have approved plans by the local Council or Private Certifier. If there is an extension without approved plans, this may cause issues for you with the local Council in the future.
- Check if there is any possibility of termites or asbestos.

- What is the immediate maintenance required to live in the house?
- Nearby transportation, schools and shopping facilities.
- If a tenant is currently occupying the house and you are buying to live in it, check with the agent when the lease will expire or when it will be available for vacant possession.
- If you are buying as an investment, check the current rental market. The current tenant could be paying high rent as they may have been living in the property for a number of years. You should consider that if the property falls vacant then you may get a new tenant at a reduced rental rate.

Always take your time during an inspection even though there may be other people doing the same. You should not be put off if the house is unclean or untidy as this is just a cosmetic issue. Ensure that you take notes of any maintenance and upgrades that you may need to do.

It is also important to find out how long the property has been on the market. Sometimes a property may be on the market for several months and this should alarm you that there could be potential serious issues. It may be that there is something physically wrong with the property, it's overpriced or some other issue.

Buying Properties off the Plan

Buying properties off the plan is when you decide to buy a property that is yet to be constructed or is still under construction. There are advantages and disadvantages when proceeding in this direction.

Advantages

- Price: There is a possibility at the final completion of the property that the price may have increased.
- The settlement period will be as long as until the property is finally built.

Disadvantages

- The value of the property may drop while under construction or when completed. If so, you will pay more than the current market value. This may cause problems with the lending institution who is providing the loan as the property value has gone down which means you may have to fork out the shortfall in the loan during the settlement.
- Building plans can change during construction. You need to verify the percentage of variation and if there is room for negotiation on the price.
- There could be delays in the completion date. You need to check the contract of sale for when the developer was scheduled to finish the construction.

NOTE: Before entering into a contract to buy off the plan, always obtain relevant legal advice.

Making an Offer

Making an offer is an important aspect of the buying process but note an offer should be made from a financial point of view and not with your emotions. There will always be another day, another property, and another offer that you could make, so it is not the end of the world if your offer is not accepted.

Before making an offer, you should take the following into account:

- Estimate the cost of any maintenance required on the property.
- Review other similar properties in the same price range and what they were sold for. This will not be exact but at least it will give you a relevant comparison.
- Ensure your loan has been pre-approved.
- If the listed price is $869k, you should not be making an offer of $869k but something lower than that.
- In terms of financial capacity, you must get your sums right when making the

offer. Take into account the offer price plus other costs that you may have to pay, including stamp duty and solicitor's fees.

Once you have determined acceptable answers to these questions, you can make an offer in writing or verbally, depending on the real estate agent's advice. You may receive one of three possible responses:

- Yes, the offer is accepted
- No, the offer is rejected
- Update your offer or renegotiate the offer to come to an agreed price.

If you receive a response to renegotiate, be sure to remain within your budget. Sometimes, while negotiating with a seller, you may become emotional about buying the property and go over your budget. How much leeway you have depends on how much you can stretch in your negotiation. Remember, always keep your offer as low as possible.

Caution – If the agent or the vendor cannot come to an agreed price and they stick to the price they want, and you sincerely feel that it is not worth changing your offer, then walk away. Never be pressurised into a deal when you are not comfortable or do not agree. **There will always be the next deal, you just need perseverance and patience.**

If the response is yes, you will need to pay a holding deposit of 0.25% and sign the contract with a 5-10 days cooling off period during which the searches are conducted and the contract is read by your solicitor.

Special Conditions in the Contract

It is important that you go through and read the contract thoroughly before paying the 0.25% holding deposit and signing the contract. Usually, your solicitor will receive the contract after you have signed it and paid the 0.25% holding deposit.

Release of Deposit

This special condition provides the release of the 10% deposit to the vendor before the settlement if requested.

In normal circumstances, the deposit is held by the real estate agent and is only released upon the final settlement.

If the deposit is released to the vendor before the final settlement, there is a potential risk of not recovering the deposit if the following occur:

- Vendor is bankrupt
- Vendor's death
- There are legal disputes regarding the property
- There are issues arising from the vendor's mortgagee (e.g., if the sale price does not cover the total outstanding mortgage).

In my experience regarding the release of the 10% deposit, I have requested my solicitor to send a request to the vendor's solicitor to remove this clause to safeguard my interest and to reduce the possibility of losing my deposit if for any reason the settlement does not proceed.

This request or mutual arrangement should be made before paying the 0.25% holding deposit and signing the contract.

If the vendor turns down the request to remove the release of the 10% deposit clause before the settlement, then you have an option not to proceed. If you have already paid the 0.25%, then you will lose this holding deposit if you opt out during the cooling off period.

Note: Before paying the 10% deposit, you must ensure that your loan is approved and also advise the lending body that you have signed off the contract and will be paying a 10% deposit. It is also advisable to send a copy of the signed contract to the lending body through your solicitor.

Signing Off on a Contract

Once the offer has been made and the vendor accepts the offer, you will be required to sign the contract and pay the holding deposit of 0.25% of the offer price within 5-10 business days of the cooling off period. Before signing the contract, it is advisable to inform your solicitor regarding the prospective purchase. The holding deposit of 0.25% is a non-refundable deposit if you rescind the contract for any reason.

Once the 0.25% holding deposit has been paid, the signed contract will be forwarded to your solicitor. During the 5-10 days cooling off period the solicitor will read the contract and arrange for some searches to investigate whether there are any encumbrances on the property and that all other conditions have been met. The solicitor will make an appointment to discuss and highlight any issues or concerns with you.

If buying a unit or apartment, it is also advisable to request a strata report. The strata report will detail the maintenance report of the block of units, sinking fund, details of previous strata minutes, and if there are any potential asbestos concerns. During this cooling off period, it is also important to advise your lending institution of the purchase of the property so they get the ball rolling, even though the loan has been pre-approved.

Paying the 10% Deposit

If you and the solicitor are satisfied with the contract and the reports do not show any defects, you will be required to pay a deposit of 10% of the contract price. If you do not wish to use cash to pay the deposit, you could request your bank to issue a bank guarantee.

The bank guarantee means that the bank will ensure the deposit of the buyer will be met. In the event if the buyer defaults to settle, the bank will honour the required amount as stated on the bank guarantee.

To obtain a bank guarantee, the purchaser needs to contact the bank and request for a bank guarantee. The buyer will complete the application to nominate the amount and reasons for the bank guarantee.

Post Cooling off Period

After a 10% deposit has been paid, the purchaser is legally attached to the contract.

If the buyer pulls out after the exchange of the contract, the seller can then rescind the contract and keep any deposit paid. The vendor can also resell the property and may claim any losses that would have occurred.

NOTE: It is therefore very important to confirm the loan and final assessment of your financial capabilities with the bank before paying the 10% deposit and the cooling-off period expires.

In the meantime, the buyer needs to follow up with the bank and solicitor about the final settlement to ensure it will settle as prescribed in the contract.

Final Inspection

The buyer should conduct a final inspection before the settlement takes place to ensure all fixtures, fittings, and condition of the property are the same as per pre-signing of the contract.

Buyers' contribution

The buyer should arrange for any additional contribution or payment required as part of the settlement to be forwarded onto the solicitor. The most common payments are:

- Part of the 20% deposit to be paid by the buyer.
- Deferred stamp duty to be paid.
- Any legal cost pending to be paid to the solicitor.

The buyer should request the settlement schedule from the solicitor days before the settlement to ensure all costs and amounts are correct as agreed by the bank and the solicitor.

Settlement

It takes around 42 days for the settlement of the property. Keep in touch with your solicitor and lending body to ensure the settlement will be completed as scheduled.

The final inspection should be arranged before the property settlement to ensure all fixtures, fittings and condition of the property are the same as at the time of when the contract was signed.

After Settlement

Once the settlement has been completed, some important issues need to be considered:

- Obtain a final schedule of the settlement from the solicitor, irrespective of whether it is for your home or an investment property. This will be helpful for tax purposes if it is an investment property that you sell in the future.
- If it is a home you will live in, you will need an insurance cover for the building and home contents.
- Health and safety for you and your family are paramount. You may need to arrange for pest control and cleaning work to be done depending on the age of the property.

- Sanitising the house.
- With an investment property, you will need to have landlord's insurance which will cover loss of rent, malicious damage, and accidental damage to the property.
- Review the real estate management fee and read the terms and condition of the agency agreement. You may also need to consider whether you need to change the managing agent.
- Review the current rental rate paid by the tenant and whether it is in line with the current rental market rate.
- For a unit or apartment, ensure you receive the strata minutes and are up to date with the strata payments.
- Ensure all accounts for utilities and rates have your correct address.

PART 2 – INTEREST ON MORTGAGES

5. INTEREST ON LOANS

Interest Rate

Home loan owners and investors will be offered a choice of interest rate by a financial institution. Some of the types of interest rates available are:

Fixed Interest Rate

Most lenders offer loans at a fixed rate which are generally for a term of 1-5 years.

At the conclusion of each term, the interest rate usually converts to a variable rate unless another fixed term is negotiated.

Advantages:

Fixed interest rates are better for the borrower during the period when the variable interest rate is on a rising trend. You'll have a fixed repayment amount during the fixed interest term irrespective of any increase in interest rate.

Disadvantages:

When variable interest rates are on a downward trend, it may come to a point where you are paying more interest under the fixed term than if you were paying under a variable rate.

With some financial institutions, you may need to check whether there are limits to making additional payments towards the loan if it's under a fixed interest rate. The borrower will need to pay a penalty if they wish to switch from a fixed rate to a variable rate.

Also, if you wish to refinance your loan then you may be liable to pay a penalty to break the fixed term.

Variable Interest Rate

Variable interest rates are adopted by many borrowers. Banks and financial institutions set their own interest rate and could change the rate anytime depending on the market or the various products they offer.

Irrespective of the Reserve Bank's decision to increase or decrease interest rates, banks and financial institutions will have the final decision on how many basis points the interest rate is to be increased or reduced.

Advantages:

With a variable interest rate loan, you can make any amounts of additional payment apart from the principal and interest payment.

There is no penalty for making additional repayments on your loan. You could pay off your loan earlier if you keep making additional payments.

If you wish to refinance your loan, there is no penalty as you are not locked in a fixed term.

Disadvantages:

If there is a rising trend in interest rate for a lengthy period of time, then your loan repayment amount will increase. This may cause financial hardship if you had not anticipated additional loan repayments.

Split Mortgage Product

A split mortgage product is a loan feature that will enable you to split your home loan or investment loan into several accounts that can have various interest rates.

A split mortgage product may be comprised of:

- Fixed interest rate
- Variable interest rate

As discussed earlier, a fixed interest rate will allow you to choose a competitive rate that you can lock into for several years irrespective of interest rate rises.

A split mortgage product enables the borrower to manage the movements or fluctuations of interest rates during the uncertain economic climate, providing greater flexibility and security.

Advantages of a Split Mortgage Product

A split mortgage product home loan provides the following benefits:

- Interest Rates – gives you an upper hand to negotiate the best fixed interest rate and maintain the variable rate as well.
- Additional Payment – allows you to make extra payments towards the home loan against the variable component.
- Uncertainty – during the years of an uncertain economic climate where it is difficult to predict whether the interest rate will rise or fall, the split mortgage product may give borrowers some peace of mind and lower the risk factor it may pertain in future.
- Various Fixed Terms – allows you to split your loan with various fixed terms.

Example: Total loan is $500,000. The split may be:

$200,000 for 3 years @ 2.50%

$100,000 for 2 years @ 2.25%

$100,000 for 1 year @ 2.00%

$100,000 @ the variable rate

Introductory Interest Rates

Some financial institutions may also offer introductory interest rates to borrowers. An introductory rate is a special rate that is lower than the standard variable rate and is offered for a limited period only (typically around 1-2 years). After the conclusion of the bonus period, the interest rate reverts to the standard variable rate.

Advantage:

Since the rate is lower than the standard variable rate, there is a substantial saving which could help reduce the loan faster.

Disadvantage:

After the specified period, the introductory offer will revert to the standard variable rate so you should be prepared to meet the additional interest payments.

Interest-Only Payment Home Loan

The interest-only home loan is where you only pay the interest and do not pay off any of the principal component of the loan.

This term is usually for 3-5 years or could be renegotiated with your lender. Your mortgage payment will be much lower compared to an interest plus principal mortgage payment option.

An interest-only loan is usually a short-term option that gives temporary relief to home owners or investors. It is not generally considered for a prolonged period of time as no principal repayment means the total loan of the term remains static.

Example: If you borrowed $500,000 and are paying interest-only for five years, your principal amount owing will still be $500,000.

Before you proceed with the option of an interest-only loan you must carefully consider the advantages and disadvantages.

Advantages:

The mortgage holder will have a reduced repayment amount. This gives an investor the upper hand in terms of cash flow advantages. The investor may use this cash available to pay for other expenses associated with the rental property or utilise the cash available against their home loan.

Interest-only loans are also attractive for taxation purposes as you can claim the interest against your disposable income.

Disadvantages:

A higher interest amount is paid during the term of the loan as you are not paying back the principal component, therefore the loan is not being reduced as it would normally be if you were on a principal plus interest payment loan option.

When the interest only term expires you will be up for a higher payment as the loan will rollover to principal plus interest.

The property will not have much equity as the principal amount is not being paid. In this case, equity will only be generated when the property's market value increases.

PART 3 – INVESTMENT PROPERTY

6. BUYING AN INVESTMENT PROPERTY

There are many resources available about property investing for prospective investors. You may attend investment seminars, read books or magazines, or reach out to someone you know with experience.

You will hear many ideas floated such as buying a house for investment is better than a unit or apartment, or a certain area is better to buy for a higher rental yield/return, or discussions about whether positive gearing is better than negative gearing. In hindsight, can anyone identify that all those who bought a unit or apartment instead of a house have made the wrong investment decision or vice versa?

The point to make here is that every investment decision should be based on an individual's financial capacity, affordability, objective and confidence. It is wise to seek and evaluate professional advice, but the final decision is always yours.

Realised and Unrealised Gain

You may hear the term realised or unrealised gain, to summarise this means:

Realised Gain – The rental income generated from the property.

Unrealised Gain – The market value or the capital gain of the property, it is a paper-based gain. The gain is only attained and realised when the property is sold.

Example – The property was bought for $400,000 and after period of three years its market value is estimated to be $500,000. The unrealised gain will be $100,000 and can only be materialised if the property is sold for $500,000. This cannot be taken for granted since it is dependent on what the market dictates at the point of sale and what the buyer pays.

Buying a Unit/Apartment

The process of buying a unit or apartment and the things to look out for follow on from what we discussed in chapter 4. For investment purposes, there are a few additional considerations:

- Purchasing a unit is generally cheaper than buying a house.
- Owning a unit requires you to pay strata management fees every quarter. The strata management will use the fee paid for the upkeep of common areas of the property that fall under strata laws. Bigger apartment complexes with modern facilities such as elevators, swimming pools or gyms will definitely drive the strata fees up. There could also be supplementary strata levies if major works are to be done within the complex.
- The potential obligation to pay land tax is reduced as there are several other units or apartments to compensate for it.

- It is more viable for investors to enter the property market by buying a unit or apartment than buying a house due to the price difference.
- Units may offer a higher rental yield and greater cash flow due to the lower purchase price of the property.
- There is normally less personal outdoor space for families, but some complexes may have additional shared facilities.
- Many units or apartments are constructed near city centres or metropolitan areas which are usually closer to transport, schools, restaurants and other facilities.
- Any major renovations to be done within the complex require approval from the strata management.

Buyer's Checklist:

- Size of the unit/apartment including bedroom spaces.
- Condition of the bathroom.
- Condition of the kitchen.

- Does it have built-ins?
- Does it have air-conditioning?
- Does it have an internal laundry?
- Does it have a balcony?
- Does it need painting?
- Floor conditions.
- What are the other facilities within the complex?
- Parking facilities, is it a lockup garage or car space?
- What are the surrounding areas and facilities such as transportation, school and shopping facilities?
- Read the strata minutes if available and review the current building condition, current maintenance works, potential asbestos and whether the sinking fund is sufficient (additional levy fees may be raised to ensure the sinking fund is sufficient for maintenance works).
- Review the current rental market rate in comparison to what the tenant is currently paying. For example, if the tenant is paying more than the current rental market then you are at an advantage. If

you are planning to renovate the property after purchasing then carefully consider when to do it as you don't want to vacate a property for renovation and then re-tenant it at a lower rental market rate or struggle to get a tenant at all if the current rental climate happens to be in over supply.

Buying a House

Buying a house is similar to buying a unit or apartment, however there are a few differences as well to consider:

- Buying a house is usually more expensive than buying a unit.
- No strata payment is required.
- Houses may have greater scope for sourcing tenants as those with larger families and spending capacity may look to acquire a bigger space.
- Water usage can be claimed from the tenant with a separate meter.

- The land value will appreciate over time, posing a potential obligation to pay for land tax. Land tax is dependent on the value and number of other properties you may already have (not including your residential property).
- Council rates are higher for houses than units or apartments in a given particular suburb.
- All maintenance is carried out by the landlord (you, as the owner).
- Houses will normally offer a higher capital growth because of the land component of the property. This may be an advantage to high-end investors who wish to offset the negative gearing loss against their disposable income (salary and wage earners).
- There is a private outdoor space for families and so the tenant does not need to share any additional facilities including outdoor entertainment areas.
- You may renovate at your own will as there is no strata body approval to gain.

Buyer's Checklist:

- Size of the house and number of bedrooms.
- Condition of the bathroom.
- Condition of the kitchen.
- Are there easements on the property?
- Is there any extension to the original property? You should be able to find approved plans from the local Council. If an extension does not have approved plans, then you may be subject to fines or penalties or demolition of the extension by the local council in future.
- Is there a possibility of termites or asbestos?
- What immediate maintenance works are required for a tenant to live in the house?
- Research the area for transportation, schools and shopping facilities.
- If the tenant is currently occupying the house you are buying to live in, check with the agent when the lease would expire or when it will be available for vacant possession.

- Review the current rental market in comparison to what the tenant is currently paying. If the tenant is paying more than the current rental market rate, you should carefully consider whether you will get the same rental return if the property falls vacant.

Types of Ownership

There are various types of ownership structures to consider when purchasing a property:

Single Ownership

The property has one owner and there is one name on the title deed. The owner has full ownership of the property.

Joint Tenant

The property is owned in equal share with another person and both have full ownership of the property. In the event where one owner dies, the surviving person is entitled to the full share of the property.

Tenancy in Common

The property has two or more persons owning the property. During the tenancy in common ownership, if an event occurs where one owner dies, the ownership of that person's share will form part of the other owner's estate. Each ownership share can have equal shares or unequal shares. For example, three owners of the property may have unequal shares of 10%, 30% and 60%.

There are other types of ownership that can be chosen such as trust ownership and company ownership. You will need to seek professional advice about these structures before deciding if they are suitable for you.

7. INVESTMENT INCOME

Rental Yield

When you are thinking of investing, there are certain factors that an investor will look into before deciding to buy an investment property. One factor you should understand is the rental yield, as this becomes an important tool for investors. In simple terms, rental yield is the income generated from an investment property. This is expressed as a percentage of the value of the investment.

There is no fixed rule of thumb to determine a single percentage that represents a good potential yield. As a guide, one may take an average of 3-6%. However, the rental yield should be considered on a case-by-case basis, depending on the value of the property.

There are two types of rental yield that can be calculated to ascertain the property's potential: *Gross Rental Yield and Net Rental Yield.*

Gross Rental Yield

Gross rental yield may be defined as annual rental income against the value of the property. There are several methods to increase the rental yield of your investment property such as:

- Limit expenses.
- Ensure your property is not vacant for a long period of time as this will affect your rental income.
- Ensure the rental rate is aligned with the current market price.
- Research before buying the investment property, look for an area that has potential rental growth.

Table 2 – *Gross rental yield calculation*

GROSS RENTAL YIELD	Per Annum
Rent - $580.00 per week	$30,160
Property value	$700,000
Gross Yield	4.31%

Table 2 shows the gross rental yield percentage method, based on the total rent per annum divided by the property value and multiplied by 100.

So, Gross Rental Yield = (Annual Rent $30,160 / Property Value $700,000) x 100.

Net Rental Yield

Net rental yield is the annual rental minus annual expenses against the value of the property. Table 3 shows some of the expenses to consider which relate to generating rental income.

Table 3 – Net rental yield calculation

NET RENTAL YIELD	Per Annum
Rent @ $580.00 per week	$30,160
Rates	$1,200
Water	$700
Insurance	$800
Repairs and maintenance	$1,500
Management fees @ 5.5%	$1,659
Net income	$24,301
Property value	$700,000
Net Yield	3.47%

The net rental yield percentage method is based on the total rent per annum, less annual expenses divided by the property value and multiplied by 100.

So, Net Rental Yield = (Annual Rent minus Annual Expenses $24,301 / Property Value $700,000) x 100.

NOTE – The higher the property value, the lower the estimated rental yield. Or, if your property is undervalued, you will have a higher rental yield.

When purchasing an investment property, the real estate agent may advertise the rental yield to attract investors. You should also calculate the yield yourself and compare the rental market with properties similar to the property you are considering for purchase. It is also important to assess whether you will be able to attract tenants with the same rental rate if the current tenant moves out.

Table 4 shows the yield difference if the rental income changes. Suppose you bought a property with rental income generating $580.00 per week with a gross rental yield of 4.31% and a net rental yield of 3.47% (see tables 2 & 3). Then, suppose the tenant moves out and you are unable to attract the same rental rate, for example, you may get a new tenant who will pay $500.00 per week. Hence your gross rental yield is 3.71% and your net rental yield is 2.91% (see table 4). This shift or reduction may be due to economic factors and lower rental demand or due to the previous tenant having paid more rent for a convenient location or other benefit.

Table 4 – Impact of rental income changes

GROSS RENTAL YIELD	Per Annum
Rent - $500.00 per week	$26,000
Property value	$700,000
Gross Yield	3.71%

NET RENTAL YIELD	Per Annum
Rent @ $500.00 per week	$26,000
Rates	$1,200
Water	$700
Insurance	$800
Repairs and maintenance	$1,500
Management fees @ 5.5%	$1,430
Net income	$20,370
Property value	$700,000
Net Yield	2.91%

8. PROPERTY GEARING

Positively Geared Property

Positive gearing occurs when the rental income is greater than all-associated costs of managing the property such as mortgage repayments, rates, strata fees, property management fee, repairs and maintenance, etc.

Example of a Positively Geared Property

Suppose you intend to buy an investment property for $700,000 and the property is returning $550.00 per week. The actual mortgage is $560,000 after paying a 20% deposit. Assume you have a fixed interest rate mortgage rate of 2.9% per annum.

Table 5 shows a positively geared property with a net cash flow and estimated annual income of $7,030 which equates to $136 per week.

Table 5 – Positively geared property

	Annual
Mortgage	$560,000
Rental Income ($550.00 per week)	$28,600
Interest per annum (2.90% of $560K)	$16,240
Insurance	$800
Council Rates	$1,600
Repairs and maintenance	$1,500
Management fees @ 5%	$1,430
Net income	$7,030

Advantages of a Positive Gearing Property:

- To purchase another investment property. You would be building equity in your property which is an advantage when seeking an additional loan.
- Risk avoidance. You tend to minimise your investment risk in the event of unforeseen circumstances such as losing your job. In this instance, all your expenses including the interest repayment will be covered by the rental income. Depending on the percentage of positive gearing, this

additional income may be handy during a difficult time.

- Retirement. An investor who is near retirement will not want out-of-pocket expenses. Instead, they can rely on their positively geared property for income.
- First-time investors. First-time investors who enter the market may prefer to have a positive cash flow to give them peace of mind so that they don't run into a situation where they have to be out-of-pocket and struggle to meet mortgage repayments and expenses.

Disadvantages of a Positive Gearing Property:

- Tax implications. Any income or profit derived from the investment is taxable income, so you are liable to pay tax along with any disposable income from other sources such as wages or salaries.

Negatively Geared Property

Negative gearing occurs when the rental income is less than all-associated costs of managing the property such as mortgage repayments, rates, strata fees, property management fee, repairs and maintenance, etc.

There will always be a shortfall and the investor will be out-of-pocket to meet the mortgage repayment and property expenses. The negative geared property in financial terms will incur a loss. This loss can be claimed and offset against your other income during that year which will reduce your tax payable.

Example of a Negatively Geared Property

Suppose you intend to buy an investment property for $950,000 and the property is returning $650.00 per week with a fixed interest rate mortgage of 2.9% per annum.

Table 6 shows a negatively geared property with a net loss and estimated annual loss of $4,040 which equates to $78 per week.

Table 6 – Negatively geared property

	Annual
Mortgage	$950,000
Rental Income ($650.00 per week)	$33,800
Interest per annum (2.90% of $950K)	$27,550
Insurance	$1,200
Council Rates	$2,400
Repairs and maintenance	$5,000
Management fees @ 5%	$1,690
Net Loss	-$4,040

Advantages of a Negative Gearing Property:

- Tax implications. Negative gearing is a loss on your rental property during the financial year and may offset against other income earned, such as your wages or salaries. This reduces your taxable income and tax payable.
- High growth areas. Some areas where properties are more expensive may result in negative gearing however these areas may have higher growth potential. In this case, you will have good capital growth

where in the long term the total costs incurred could offset when the property is eventually sold for a higher price.

- Increase in equity. High growth areas tend to have great potential for an increase in capital growth. This increases the property's equity and gives a greater borrowing power when adding another property to your investment portfolio.

Disadvantages of a Negative Gearing Property:

It is important to understand the risks and not fall prey to the misconception that buying an investment property is to reduce your tax by negative gearing. This strategy may not work for everyone. For some, property investments are treated as an income generating business and for any business you do not want to run at a loss every year.

- Higher risk. You tend to be in a higher investment risk category, especially if you lose your job or if your financial situation deteriorates due to unforeseen circumstances. You will need to have a backup plan to meet out-of-pocket expenses.

- Passive income. If you are near retirement age, this strategy may not be viable. You will not receive passive income or be able to offset the loss of negative gearing against your disposable income as you will not be earning much from your regular stream of income.
- Cash flow drain out. Under negative gearing, there will always be an out-of-pocket expense, unless there is a gradual increase in rent, decrease in interest on mortgage or a reduction on expenses.

Before embarking on buying an investment property, one must consider the outlay of funds required, including the deposit, associated costs, and the expected rental rate.

The three scenarios in table 7 show the total cost to service an investment property loan and indicate the differences between three different deposits of 5%, 10%, or 20%. The lower the deposit, the higher the loan repayment will be.

This scenario is based on an interest-only repayment for an investment property with a fixed interest rate of 2.5% for two years. After two years, the rate will revert to a variable rate which could be higher than the initial fixed rate.

When purchasing a property, you will have upfront costs such as legal costs and stamp duty. If these are included in the loan amount, the total repayment will be much higher.

Table 7 illustrates the approximate costs to be paid on a weekly basis for an interest only loan after paying a deposit of 5%, 10% or 20%. Other costs of owning a property will include council rates, water rates, strata fees, real estate management fees and an estimate for miscellaneous costs such as repairs and maintenance. This will enable you to determine whether you will be out-of-pocket (negative gearing) or whether you will save (positive gearing) against the weekly rent that you will receive.

Table 7 – Interest only weekly payment guideline

Interest rate figures are based on pre-inflation increase.

Purchase Price	20% Deposit	Net Loan	2YR Fixed Interest 2.50%	Weekly Mortgage Payment	Weekly Other Cost	Total Weekly Cost
400,000	80,000	320,000	8,000	154	161	315
450,000	90,000	360,000	9,000	173	161	334
500,000	100,000	400,000	10,000	192	161	353
550,000	110,000	440,000	11,000	212	161	373
600,000	120,000	480,000	12,000	231	161	392

Purchase Price	10% Deposit	Net Loan	2YR Fixed Interest 2.50%	Mortgage Payment	Other Cost	Total Weekly Cost
400,000	40,000	360,000	9,000	173	161	334
450,000	45,000	405,000	10,125	195	161	356
500,000	50,000	450,000	11,250	216	161	377
550,000	55,000	495,000	12,375	238	161	399
600,000	60,000	540,000	13,500	260	161	421

Purchase Price	5% Deposit	Net Loan	2YR Fixed Interest 2.50%	Mortgage Payment	Other Cost	Total Weekly Cost
400,000	20,000	380,000	9,500	183	161	344
450,000	22,500	427,500	10,688	206	161	367
500,000	25,000	475,000	11,875	228	161	389
550,000	27,500	522,500	13,063	251	161	412
600,000	30,000	570,000	14,250	274	161	435

9. PROPERTY LEASING

Renting/Leasing the Property

Irrespective of whether you choose to buy a house or a unit/apartment for investment purposes, you will need to rent out the property and so a critical part of renting is appointing a managing agent.

Within the property's local area, there will be various agents who look after many rental properties. Note, the key word here is *local*. Ideally, you want an agent is familiar with the area and the market trends in that area.

There are various points to consider when appointing a managing agent:

- Source out two or three managing agents and research their business.
- How much are their property management fees?

- Is there a lock-in term during the management agency period?
- What other services are being provided. apart from managing the property?
- How will the property be marketed and where will it be advertised to maximise exposure and the number of applications seeking to rent so you can get the best tenant?
- Does the agent provide a maintenance service?
- Who is the main point of contact at the managing agent and how easy is it to get in contact with them? Do they have an office or operate remotely?
- What is the size of their rental property portfolio?
- How many property officers and managers do they have?
- What is the process for screening prospective tenants and what relevant checks are conducted before placing a tenant?

- How often is a property inspection conducted and what are the fees or charges associated with the inspection?
- Cost of the end-of-year rental statement?
- What is the protocol if the tenant falls behind on rent?
- How do they deal with difficult tenants and what are the processes involved and legal avenues available?
- How accommodating is the prospective managing agent to you as a landlord?
- Do they work in the best interest of you as a landlord as well as the tenant or do they favour the tenant over you?
- When is the rental appraisal and rent increase undertaken? The managing agent should independently determine the market rental rate for your property. Since they manage other properties in the area, they should have relevant expertise and knowledge of what your property can achieve or an appropriate rental rate.

Once you have decided on a managing agent, you, as the landlord, have obligations to ensure the safety of the tenant and anyone visiting your rented property. You need to keep tab on the lease expiry and review the rent as per the current rental market demand.

Owner's Responsibility and Action

- Ensure the property is fitted with smoke alarms that have been tested annually by certified personnel.
- The property should be covered with public liability insurance. If it is a unit, it is also advisable to have landlord insurance which should cover the contents, loss of rent, and malicious damage or accidental incidents.
- Always be prompt in attending to any maintenance work required as some may be of great urgency such as electrical or plumbing issues.
- Determine the duration of the lease and whether you want the tenant to enter a long-term or short-term lease. Generally, if possible with a new tenant, it is advisable to enter only a six-months lease,

as you are not fully aware of the capabilities and the nature of the tenant. However, this may differ depending on your jurisdiction.

- You should inspect the property at least twice a year or per the recommended advice in your state to ensure the property is kept in good condition. It is important to give immediate attention to any maintenance required to avoid further deterioration of the property.
- Act swiftly if the tenant defaults on rent and investigate their financial situation or hardship.

Tradespeople Appointed by Agents

During the period when the property is being managed by the agent, they may recommend that you use their tradespeople.

In some cases, you may use the tradespeople appointed by the agent if the matter is urgent and needs immediate attention but with other non-urgent matters, it would be in your best interest to get another quote. This will give you an indication of the current market rate for that particular job. Remember, you do not want the maintenance cost to be inflated because this is your investment property.

It is very important to obtain at least three quotes. You will be surprised by how different some quotes can be for a similar job. From time to time, you will come across some tradespeople who will try to squeeze extra dollars from you, especially if they know you are an "investor".

You should also remember that whenever a tradesperson conducts repairs and maintenance to the property, you must ensure that you check yourself or through a trusted person that the work has been completed and cross-check against the written quote so that you are sure all works have been completed as per the agreement.

Finding a Tenant

When selecting an agent to market your property for lease, ensure you are aware of their strategies and efforts:

- Are they only doing open homes once or twice a week or is it also by request when prospective tenants are available to inspect the property? If the strategy is based on the open home time only, then chances are you may miss an opportunity to attract tenants who may wish to inspect on other days.
- When the first inspection is conducted, you will see prospective tenants come and submit an application to lease the property. The agent may suggest holding the applications and waiting for another week or two. You should be mindful that prospective tenants may not wait for you and may sign off elsewhere by the time the agent contacts them again.
- Ensure you are given feedback on the next day about how many people attended and how many took an application form.

- Any application forms received by the agent should be attended to immediately by checking their rental history, salary or wage evidence, and details of the occupants that will be living in the property.

Renovating a Property

When undertaking renovation before or after leasing a property, there are several important factors to consider:

1. **Market trends**. If the market trend shows housing prices are falling, consider all pros and cons of the type of renovations you will be undertaking.

If you are renovating a property to sell in the falling price market or if you have over-capitalised on renovation, you may not get value for money as you may have spent more than your expected sale price.

2. **Overcapitalising.** Different types of property will have different needs and services. If you are renovating your family home, you would do it differently than if you are renovating an investment property.

Renovating a Family Home: You will renovate based on your own taste and choices, which may be an expensive affair, especially if you plan to live in this property for several years to get the long-term benefit of your investment when you sell.

Renovating an Investment Property: You will have tenants come and go during the tenure of the property. Renovation will be based on the current economic climate and your financial capacity, not on your emotions. Your renovation should be very practical, and a financial assessment must be done to keep in mind of the rental yield you would achieve once the renovation is complete. Fixtures and fittings should be practical for the everyday tenant's needs.

3. **Obtaining a loan to renovate.** This will require a thorough assessment of the renovation and so investors need to be confident that they will get a higher rental yield after the renovation. You should also consider whether the rental market is rising, flat or in a downward trend.

4. **Do-it-yourself renovations.** Some investors have skills to perform some renovation tasks. It is important to note that some jobs must be completed by qualified personnel, such as electrical and plumbing. Some tasks that can easily be performed by the owner could be painting, tiling, and other minor works.

5. **Approval required.** If the renovations have a substantial budget, you may need to get approval from your local council or strata management. You may also require works to be carried out by a licenced builder due to the work cost rising above a specific threshold.

6. **Renovation by builder.** If you choose a builder or various tradespeople to do all or part of the renovation, you should ensure they are all licensed. You can verify the status of the builder's or tradesperson's licence on the Fair Trading website or the equivalent organisation for your state. Always obtain a written quote from the tradesperson or builder before the job is undertaken and, when the job is completed, ensure that you are provided with a tax invoice and proper warranty (e.g., for electrical installation).

7. **Work health & safety.** All renovation and building works should be covered with relevant insurances including public liability insurance, irrespective of whether you are doing it yourself or with a builder or tradespeople. Public Liability Insurance covers your liability for injuries to another person or damage to their property. There is a likelihood of being sued for negligence or an unpredictable accident, which could be costly. This insurance may cover you

for negligent acts that cause personal injury or property damage. You can obtain more information about public liability insurance from insurance companies and the state legislation.

PART 4 – SELLING PROPERTY

10. PROPERTY SALES

Deciding to Sell your Property

A residential property may be the most important asset that you will have acquired and have spent your life savings on to purchase. When you intend to sell, it is a big decision, irrespective of whether it's your family home or an investment property.

There are various methods to sell your property and a real estate agent will be able to guide you. Common methods include:

- Private Treaty
- Auction
- Expression of Interest

Private Treaty

Private treaty sale is when the home-owner and real estate agent set a price for the property.

The property will be marketed at this price and the real estate agent will negotiate with every prospective buyer who has shown an interest in your property or has made an offer.

Private treaty offers hands-on control over the sale and allows both parties some time to make an appropriate decision. As the price is listed, it is easier for buyers to determine their affordability and the listed price can be adjusted throughout the marketing stage, depending on various market conditions.

Auction

An auction is the process of selling the property with buyers bidding against each other to purchase and is organised by a licensed real estate agent or hired auctioneer.

Auctions occur on a specific day, place, and time. Before the auction, the real estate agent marketing the property will assist you to determine the reserve price (i.e., the minimum price you are willing to accept).

Expression of Interest (EOI)

Sale by EOI is a process whereby a vendor forwards an invitation to buyers to submit an offer to purchase the property. A prospective buyer will state the price they are willing to pay for the property in their submission.

The property will be on the market for a specific timeframe with a closing date for the EOI. After the closing date, each submission will be reviewed to finalise the sale.

Once you have decided to sell a property, you will need a real estate agent to market the property and sell it on your behalf.

Appointing a Real Estate Agent

Before you search for a real estate agent to give you a market appraisal, you must do your own research on the selling price of similar properties with similar features sold recently within your suburb. This will give you a better guide to the property's value in the current market and be a tool for comparison when the agent does an appraisal and gives you a listing price for your property.

Many times, it has been quite apparent that properties which are priced too low may not achieve the best result. Buyers may form the perception that there are issues with the property, based on an overly low price. At the other end of the spectrum, if the property is priced too high, it may put off buyers.

Generally, you will source at least three real estate agents to provide a market appraisal for your property.

Factors to consider when deciding to appoint an agent, may include:

- **Local real estate agent**: most vendors go with their local real estate agent because they have sold similar properties within the area.
- **Marketing strategy**: this is how the real estate agent will market and advertise your property. This is a very important aspect of selling the property which will

indicate how they are going to reach out to prospective buyers.

- **Marketing costs:** most agents charge upfront marketing costs. It is becoming more common for the vendor to absorb marketing costs irrespective of whether the property is sold or not. Marketing costs could be anything from $1,000 to $5,000 or more, depending on the real estate agent, how they market the property, and the type of property being advertised. Vendors should discuss marketing costs with their real estate agent and have a clear understanding in writing about what they will cover and how it will be used during the term of the campaign. Generally, the marketing costs for auctions will be considerably higher than for private treaty.
- **Agent commission:** agent commission is charged in addition to marketing costs and is the major cost associated with selling a property, payable at the settlement of the property sale. Be aware and ask questions about the nature of services that will be

rendered by the agent and their commission rate.

Signing Off the Agency Agreement

Apart from an auction agency agreement, there are other agreements:

- **Exclusive agency agreement:** Used for the sale of a residential property when you give exclusive rights to one agent to sell your property. The agent will be entitled to a commission, irrespective of whether the property is sold by them or by another agent during the fixed term of the agency agreement.
- **Sole agency agreements:** When you give the rights to one agent to sell the property but, if you happen to find a buyer who has not been introduced by the appointed agent, no commission is payable to the agent.
- **Open listing:** You can list your property with more than one agent and pay a

commission to the agent who finds the buyer.

Once you have decided on the type of agency agreement to proceed with, your agent will arrange to compile an agreement between you and the agency.

Irrespective of which agency agreement you have opted for, you must ensure that the document includes relevant information such as the defined period of the agreement, agency commission, price range of the property and marketing costs.

Contract of Sale

The contract of sale should be prepared before any residential property is advertised for sale.

To prepare the contract, you must engage a solicitor or a conveyancer.

Selling Family Home

Selling your family home can be for several reasons, including:

- Buying a bigger home
- Downsizing your current home
- Financial constraints in maintaining your current mortgage (affordability)

It is not advisable to disclose to agents that you have bought another property and wish to urgently sell your current property. This may work against you if the buyer and the agent are aware that you are desperate to sell to fund the other property or are in the difficult situation of holding onto two mortgages at the same time.

If they are aware of any urgency, it is possible the offers may be considerably lower than what you expected due to the assumption that you intend to sell quickly.

Selling Existing Home or Leasing it

When intending to upgrade their current home to something more spacious, most people sell and buy or build an alternative home.

When you sell your current home, there may be a short fall of funds to acquire a bigger home depending on how much was outstanding on your current home loan. If this is the case, it is wise to consider the option of leasing the current home instead of selling it.

With this strategy you can still maintain the property as an investment. You may have equity in your current home which would put you in a better position to obtain a second loan while also allowing you to receive rental income from leasing it.

Selling Investment Property

Selling an investment property may not be as emotionally draining as selling your family home, but sometimes making the decision to sell an investment property is not all that simple.

Vendors need to be comfortable and sure when selling that they have fully assessed the property market to attain the maximum capital gain, but this may not be the case if they are in dire financial constraints and have no alternative but to sell.

Most investors may keep their investment property long-term, and this may also be their retirement funding strategy. In hindsight, this may be an individual decision adopted by the investor as they may be interested in the property flipping strategy.

When selling an investment property, it is vital to understand the concept of capital gains and the tax implications of the gain you make when an investment property is sold.

There are several issues that need to be considered before selling an investment property, such as:

- How much is the property worth? A real estate agent can do the market appraisal.
- Vendor should conduct their own research to determine the likely property value by comparing recent sales of similar properties. While this may not be exact, it will give you a fair idea or a ballpark figure.
- Consider the payment of capital gains tax.
- Liaise with a real estate agent about whether to sell by private treaty or by auction.
- What is the agent's commission?
- Are there any upfront marketing costs?
- Appoint a solicitor to prepare the contract.
- Will you require vacant possession of the property or sell the property with tenants occupied.
- If the selling agent is different from the managing agent, the managing agent should be advised that the property is going onto the market.

- Tenants should be well advised with due notice on every occasion about inspection times, and if the property is sold when the settlement will take place.

Selling Property with Tenants

Buyers who are investors are much more inclined to buy a property that has tenants occupied as there is a guaranteed income flow from the day settlement takes place and they do not need to wait or advertise for a tenant.

From the vendor's perspective, the vendor will continue to receive rental income while the property is on the market. This will avoid the loss of thousands of dollars of income while waiting for the property to be sold and settlement to be completed.

The vendor's agent is required to give sufficient notice to the tenant before each inspection is undertaken by prospective buyers.

Selling Property without Tenants

Vendors are required to give ample notice to the tenant about vacating the property before it goes onto the market for sale. The period of notice to be given will depend on the conditions specified in the current lease agreement with your tenant or in accordance with the laws in your jurisdiction.

Selling a property without tenants makes it easier for the agent to show the property to potential buyers as no appointment or liaison with the tenant is required.

Some buyers would also want to occupy the property as soon as the settlement is completed if they are purchasing it as a residential home.

11. SELLING PROPERTY – EXPERIENCES

Price Ranges

Price ranges are not my preference when selling a property. In my opinion if a property is listed between $800,000 - $850,000, my immediate thought would be to offer $800,000 because why would one initially opt to pay at the higher end of the range?

For instance, the agent advises the vendor to list the property with a specific range. They also indicate that they have many buyers on their database who are looking for a similar property. The property goes on the market with the agent and on the first Saturday has a few prospective buyers but no offers. After the second inspection, the agent advises there is not much interest in the property and his recommendation is to lower the price by 20-30K and change the mode of listing from a range to a fixed price listing.

Glossy Presentations

A property is vacant when it goes on the market and the agent proposes that it is advisable to hire furniture to put in the property for presentation so that it doesn't look "small".

This practice is mostly logical and cost-effective for exclusive, spacious and brand-new properties. It also comes down to an individual choice.

Do not get carried away with glossy handouts, you must be savvy in reading and analysing the facts about the property with your basic understanding of the buying and selling process.

Market Appraisal and Offer

Market appraisals can differ amongst agents even though the property may be similar to others or unique in its own way. It is interesting to see how market appraisals can be subjective at times from person to person.

The tenant moves out and renovation is completed with an all-new kitchen, bathroom and laminated timber flooring before being viewed by a few agents for a market appraisal.

Agent 1 is already the managing agent and provided an honest assessment of the property. They did not want to hold the property on the market for too long and expected to sell quickly.

Agent 2 views the property and indicated the property is too old, kitchen is poor despite being new, no air conditioning, needs built-ins and suggests the timber flooring is second-hand.

Agent 3 views the property and gave a listing price that was slightly above my expectation. The agent seemed confident yet humble in getting a buyer.

The property was eventually sold by Agent 3 after three weeks. An offer was made to which the agent managed to get an additional sum above the offered price. The offer received was an additional 25-30K above the original expectation.

12. CAPITAL GAIN

Capital Gains Tax

When selling an investment property, you will make a gain or loss which should be reported within the annual tax return period. In most cases, when a vendor disposes or sells an investment property, there is a capital gain from the proceeds of sale.

The capital gain is the difference between the cost to acquire the property and the net gain you made when the property was sold.

It is also important to note when the capital gain should be reported. The capital gain will be calculated and reported in the financial year when the vendor signs off on the contract for sale.

Suppose the contract of sale was signed on 15/6/2020 (FY 2020) and the settlement was due on July 2020 (FY 2021), the capital gain from the sale will need to be accounted for in the financial year ending 2020 and not the financial year ending 2021.

Capital Gains Tax Discounted Method

Table 8 shows the capital gains tax payable on the assumption that you have owned the property for more than 12 months in order to be eligible for the 50% discount.

If the property had more than one ownership, then the capital gain would be divided amongst the ownership. Suppose there were two owners, the capital gains tax payable by each owner would be $53,000.

Table 8 – CGT payable using discounted method

Selling Price of Property	$950,000
Less Purchase Price of Property	$650,000
Gain on Sale	$300,000
Less Capital Gain Discount - 50%	$150,000
Less cost associated with purchase (Stamp Duty/Legal Fees, etc)	$44,000
Capital Gains Tax Payable	$106,000

Capital Gains Tax without Discounted Method

Table 9 shows the capital gains tax payable on the assumption that it includes single ownership and the property is owned for less than 12 months. In this case you are not eligible for the 50% discount.

If the property had more than one ownership, then the capital gain would be divided amongst the owners. Suppose there were two owners, the capital gains tax payable for each owner would be $128,000.

Table 9 – CGT payable without discounted method

Selling Price of Property	$950,000
Less Purchase Price of Property	$650,000
Gain on Sale	$300,000
Less cost associated with purchase (Stamp Duty/Legal Fees, etc)	$44,000
Capital Gains Tax Payable	$256,000

It is important to note the difference between tables 8 and 9. By holding the property for 12 months or more, it allows you to save a significant amount of capital gains tax.

13. PROPERTY FLIPPING

Define Flipping Strategy

Property flipping is an investment strategy that involves buying a run-down property or a low value property, renovating it, and then selling it at a profit.

To generate a higher profit, the renovation should be completed as soon as possible, and, in some cases, this may be a cosmetic renovation only. The investor should be well-versed with the renovation techniques and should be able to complete it as scheduled.

Flipping is not for every investor as it involves significant time, effort, cashflow, expertise and delivery of the project in a very limited time frame to achieve the best result.

Property flipping will attract capital gains tax and whether or not you receive the discount will depend on when you sell.

Some key factors need to be considered when looking at the buy and sell strategy:

- **Timing:** Buying properties during a period of growth in the market where it can be sold at a higher price that it was bought is beneficial.
- **Buy low and sell high:** There are properties that require quick sale due to the conditions of the property or the vendor is in urgent need of cash.
- **Negotiation skills:** You must be able to negotiate with the agent for the price you want and offer a quick settlement.
- **Firm offers:** Try and stick within your budget. Walk away if an offer falls through.
- **Redraw facility against your home loan:** It is much easier to have this facility than to apply for new loans each time you intend to flip a property. This will also avoid having the bank conduct property valuations.
- **Property structure:** Ensure the property is structurally sound if you aim to complete

only cosmetic repairs such as painting, kitchen, bathroom, flooring, etc.

- **Maintenance work:** If you can do minor works yourself, you will save on costs. Be sure to get quotes when engaging contractors and make sure works are completed on time.
- **Planning:** Planning is the key to flipping to avoid delays and exorbitant costs.
- **Upfront costs and ongoing costs:** Remember, there will be upfront costs and ongoing costs while you are in the property maintenance period:
    1. Stamp duty
    2. Legal fees
    3. Monthly interest on the loan
    4. Renovation costs
    5. Real estate agent selling fees and commission
    6. Insurance costs
    7. Capital gains tax provision (refer to chapter 12 on capital gains calculation)
- **Back-up plan:** What is the back-up plan if you are not able to sell the property at

your asking price? Can you sustain the mortgage for a longer period than anticipated or will you need to lease the property until it is sold?

There needs to be a well-planned strategy in place before embarking on a property flipping journey, especially if you are on a tight budget.

14. PROPERTY CYCLE PHASE

Housing Boom

A housing boom occurs when house prices increase dramatically and there is a disparity between the demand and supply, with many prospective buyers and not enough properties on the market.

Investing during the housing boom period

There has been a lot of debate on whether to buy during the boom period or to wait. This depends on your investment strategy and your financial stability.

If you intend to buy or invest and hold for a long period of time, then buying during a boom period may not have much negative impact on your long-term strategy in the event of a correction in the housing price.

A housing market correction is a price adjustment that occurs when there is a falling trend in house prices.

For example, if you bought a property during the boom for a short-term period, intending to sell in the near future, a correction in the housing market could lead to you losing money.

If your purchase price during the boom is $850,000 and the property is sold after the housing market correction for $790,000, then you will have a shortfall of $60,000 (excluding any associated sale and legal costs).

If you buy the same property during a boom and keep it for the-long term, say, for 10 years, the value of the property is likely to exceed beyond $850,000.

Phases in the Cycle

The property cycle is often referred to as a clock. There has been a view that this cycle lasts around 7-10 years but whether this applies in all states and territories is debated. The cycle also depends on the economic situation which could impact the length of the cycle.

The property cycle is an interesting piece of information to analyse and determine where each state or country sits in the cycle and compare it to their current economic situations. It is important to note that not all will fall into the same category at the same time.

The property cycle clock has four phases:

- Slowdown
- Slump (Buyers' Market)
- Recovery
- Boom (Sellers' Market)

It is important to analyse each phase and assess the factors contributing to it. It may be possible to predict interest movements, confidence of consumers, and the characteristic patterns of slump, slow down, recovery and boom periods.

Slowdown

- Auction clearance and private treaty sales slow down.
- Properties remain on the market for longer periods.
- Off-the-plan property prices decrease in market value after completion compared to the initial off-the-plan contract price.

Slump

- There are more sellers than buyers.
- Buyers are off the market.
- Rent becomes cheaper.
- Homeowners may default on payments.
- Mortgagee sales on the rise.
- Reserve Bank may reduce interest rates.
- Investors panic and decide to sell.
- Long term investors look for bargain sales.
- Construction of new dwellings slow down.

Recovery

- Interest rates on mortgages continue to fall.
- Fewer properties on the market.
- Rent begins to increase due to low rental vacancy.
- Credit policies may be relaxed.
- Governments announce new policies and incentives for first home buyers.
- Buyers gain confidence and start looking for properties.

Boom

- Housing prices gain momentum and begin to rise.
- More buyers as the demand for properties increase.
- Housing market reaches its peak.

Table 10 illustrates the four stages of the property market cycle and briefly states what happens in each cycle.

Table 10 – Property cycle clock

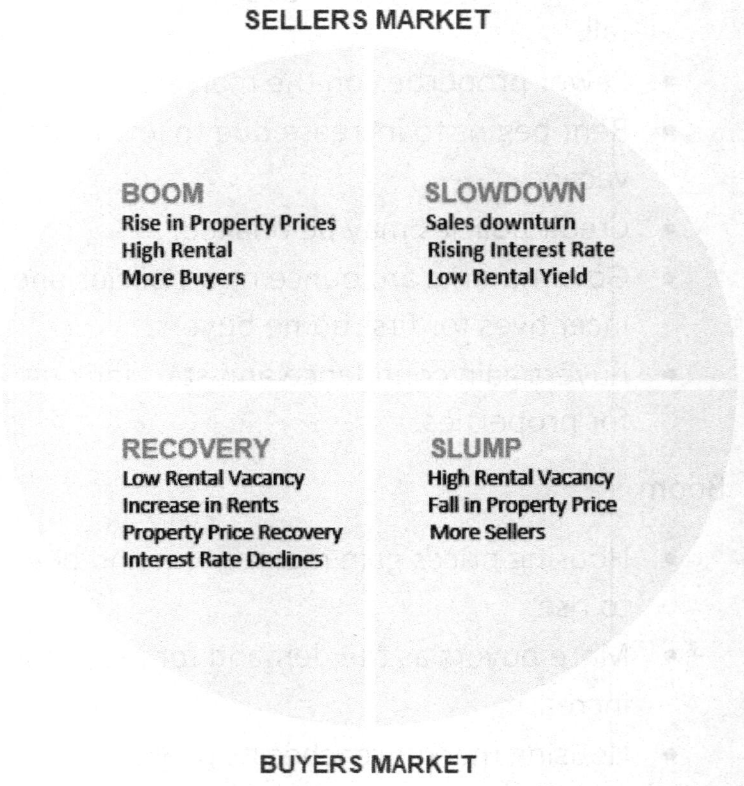

PART 5 - SHARES

15. INVESTING IN SHARES

Shares are issued to raise money for companies. There are two aspects that you may benefit from when owning shares in a company.

If a company has capital growth, your investment will increase. Suppose you bought 10,000 shares @ $1.00 and over a period the share price has increased to $1.20 per share, your capital growth is $2,000.

You may also receive dividends paid out by the company upon generating profit. However, not all companies will pay out a dividend.

Shareholders are part-owners in the company. There are two basic reasons why investors buy shares. First, to make a profit by buying at a lower price and selling at a higher price. Second, is to buy and hold shares that generate income from dividends paid by the company through their profits.

Similar to property investing, there is a financial risk in share trading. You should have a basic understanding before you trade by evaluating various factors and questions that you need to answer yourself:

Your financial capacity: Are you using your savings to invest or are you borrowing to invest? If you are borrowing to invest, you must account for the cost of interest charged on borrowing and how long you would hold onto the shares as this will have an impact on the interest that you are going to pay.

If you are using your savings to purchase shares there will be less of an impact on your financial capacity unless the shares you buy do not generate any capital gain.

Where to Invest: Depending on where you invest may lead to your success or failure. If you are a first-time investor, avoid outlaying too many funds as this could be quite risky. Your opinion should be based on the knowledge you have gained through research about the company and the past, current and potential future market conditions.

There is no correct tool or foolproof investment strategy but research will show the past trends of the share's movements, the company's current and past performances, its future goals and its strategy to achieve them.

Many investors would consider blue-chip stocks to be safer investment options. Blue-chip stocks are big companies with excellent track records that have been operating reliably for many years. They are not highly volatile and can withstand economic downturn but are also expensive to purchase and will require a large outlay. These stocks usually pay a dividend to shareholders as well.

How much to Invest: Investing a large sum of money is not good advice for many small-time or first-time investors as it means you will lock your savings in shares. Shares are regarded as a high-risk investment compared with other forms of investment such as term deposits and property investments. If there is high volatility in the market, the share price may be affected and cause you to incur heavy losses. So, if there is a low-value investment in shares, the loss will be less significant.

For example, for first-time investors it may be wise to invest a sum in the vicinity of $1,000 to $2,000 until you become comfortable and confident with share trading and familiar with stock movements and patterns.

When buying shares, you will also need to take into consideration the brokerage costs.

Borrowing funds to invest: You must be savvy enough when entering this path of borrowing money to invest. Some may borrow or use their home loan redraw facility or line of credit available within their home loan facility.

You will be paying monthly interest on these borrowed funds. With the volatility of the share market, there could be a time when you wish to cash in on your investment but if the share price has taken a dip, then you may incur a loss that could be detrimental to your financial situation.

Investment strategies

Some investment strategies may be applied per the following list but first you need to understand what type of investor you wish to be:

- Some investors would take a hands-on approach where they will be very active and oversee the movement of shares on a daily basis.
- Some investors would invest and leave the stock as it is and may contemplate on a long-term investment strategy for capital growth.
- Some would seek advice from their accredited advisers before investing.

Short-Term Trading

The trader's intention is to make a quick gain. They buy shares in anticipation of gains in the near future.

The shares in this scenario are bought in high volume so the gain will also be substantial, but this is based on speculation with some analytical research.

Although you may make a gain with this strategy, you must also consider the tax effect on the capital gain. Holding shares for longer than 12 months and then selling will make you eligible for the 50% discount on capital gains tax, but if the holding period is less than 12 months, you will pay full tax.

Long-Term Trading

Investors here put a long-term perspective on companies that are likely to incur high capital growth in the future. Investors plan carefully to invest for future wealth and longer-term retirement plans.

Research

If you wish to buy and sell shares you will need to research stock trends.

What is the company's lowest share price and highest share price? For instance, if it has not traded less than $5.00 and have not exceeded $20.00 in the last three years, then you may make a call to buy around the vicinity of $5.00 - $8.00 and sell when it's driving towards $20.00.

Preparing to Invest

Once you have decided that you are ready to invest, you will need to decide on the platform you are going to use to buy and sell shares.

Trading Platform – You will need to set up a trading platform account through a bank or financial institution. This platform will enable you to conduct trades to buy or sell, view share price movement and keep a record of your trade history. It is also important when deciding on a platform to research the trading fees.

Stockbroker – Stockbrokers can be a company or qualified individuals. They can manage your share portfolio, provide advice on your portfolio and execute various trades on your behalf.

Purchasing Stock

There are many factors that will contribute to the decision of purchasing of shares. Many first-time investors will wonder which stock to invest in. Some factors to consider are:

- Before investing, an individual should have a basic overview of investing and understand their financial capacity.
- Investigate companies that have the ability to increase in share price in the short term or longer term.
- Foresee how long you are willing to outlay funds when purchasing shares.

- Is the investment for the short term or long term?
- Have you accounted for risk factors in the event of an economic downturn?
- How many shares do you intend to purchase? Are you going to buy several small cap stocks or invest in high-value stocks?
- Research the company's growth and profitability.

It is important to research prospective companies before investing in them:

- What is the company's business (is it banking, mining, health, technology, construction, etc)?
- What are the company's profits and likely future growth? Review the company's financials and their auditor's report.
- What are the company's goals and strategies to achieve them?
- What is the company's past performances and share price movements, comparing past and present trends?

- The share price may shoot up when an announcement is made by the company about a new major partnership or an increase in sales and predicted profit. Be wary that this sudden increase in the share price may be a spontaneous, short-term market reaction.

Share Price Going Down

A common question is, what is the best action to take when the share price is going down?

Is it wise to buy when the share price is falling, assuming that in return, it will increase in the near future? Here again you cannot jump into buying the stock but should investigate the driving factors that are leading the downward trend.

The most appropriate way to verify a downward trend is by looking at the share price chart. This chart will give you an indication of whether there have been similar trends previously for a short period, how long it took to recover and whether there is a continuous falling trend in the chart.

Sometimes, shares may be overpriced, a large shareholder decides to sell their shares, a large contract is lost suggesting loss of revenue, increase in supplier costs, poor annual performance or even uncertainty in the economy, all which could cause a mass fall in share price.

A continuous falling trend in the share price in the long-term is a problem that will require you to investigate or seek professional advice before you proceed to purchase.

Selling Shares

Here, you may ask why do you wish to sell your shares, is there a strategic decision? Selling your shares needs to be carefully assessed to evaluate the reason for selling and the implication for tax disbursements. Some investors will trade into shares for short term profits only to derive a passive income from the buy-and-sell strategy.

Risk Tolerance

Risk is associated with any investment and there will always be times of higher risk. As an investor, you must decide and be clear about your level of risk tolerance when managing your portfolio.

Timing of the investment, whether it is for a short term or long-term investment, will help you understand your risk tolerance. If the share price fluctuates now but you are willing to hold onto your shares for a long period of time and are confident in the company you have invested in, then you may be more likely to recoup the short-term losses in the future and achieve higher returns in the long run.

During times of financial crisis, it all depends on the individual's risk tolerance. One of the key elements in managing risk is that you have a clear policy or mindset. It is important to not be persuaded by the emotion of others and not fall into the fear of missing out. Instead, base your decisions on facts, professional advice and analytical data.

If the share price is going down, you need to decide at what level you might sell in order to protect against the volatility of the share and the risk of the price sinking further. This depends on the number of portfolios you hold and their risk tolerance for each. Some may say 5-15%, but it also depends on the dollar value of the shares and how well your portfolio is performing overall. If all your shares are experiencing high volatility at the same time, then there is greater concern and perhaps lower risk tolerance. If your portfolio is widespread where you have invested in various industries and companies, this may ease some of the risk. In summary, there are varying levels of risk tolerance that will determine when you sell, however, there is no correct or firm answer. Ultimately, it is an individual's decision.

Tax Implications

You must be aware that when you sell your shares, you will be liable to pay tax on any capital gain arising from that transaction.

Capital Gain or Loss

A capital gain is made when an asset is sold at a profit for more than the amount you paid to acquire the asset. The amount of capital gain when selling shares is the size of the profit made by an increase in share price. You can also make a capital loss if shares are sold for less than the face value of the purchase amount.

For example, buying a stock at $1.00 per share and then selling it for $3.00 per share, would result in a capital gain of $2.00 per share. The same principle applies to a loss. Buying a stock at $2.00 per share and then selling it for $1.50 per share would result in a loss of $0.50 per share.

When to Buy/Sell

When to buy shares? There is no appropriate time as such to buy shares but many investors will look at the share movement trend.

A good example is the impact of the Covid-19 pandemic in Australia which saw billions of dollars wiped out on the stock market in late March 2020. This was an uncertain period that caused panic for many investors as they were not sure what the future would hold for share trading. But, at the same time, some investors took advantage of the downturn to invest more in the months ahead.

When to sell shares? There is no guaranteed time or rule about when to sell shares. It depends on individual circumstances and is ultimately your own decision. You may have your own exit strategy based on your research or you may be a long-term shareholder or a short-term trader.

It is quite apparent that when you have a share portfolio, not all shares will perform well or meet the expectations you may have had when you first bought them.

Coming to terms to sell your shares is sometimes very confusing but, as an investor, you should set up a benchmark for when to sell.

Example

If you purchased 50,000 in Share A @ $0.17 per share:

Share A 50,000 @ $0.17 = $8,500

Target to sell at 50% increase = $0.25

Share A 50,000 @ $0.25 = $12,500

Capital Gain = $12,500 - $8,500 = $4,000

So, you can sell once you have attained your benchmark. You must always keep in mind the implications for capital gains tax as well when setting a sell benchmark.

There may be other potential reasons that could contribute to the decision to sell your shares:

- Underperforming Shares – You may wish to dispose your shares as the share price is going down, to minimise any further losses. One should be aware that after selling the underperforming shares, suddenly the price may start to rise again. You should assess the reason for the share price trends before selling.

- Financial Constraint – An investor may have been facing financial crisis and would wish to dispose their shares.
- Sudden Share Price Increase – Some investors may want to cash in on this increase as they sense that the increase will not be permanent and the price will eventually come down. This may happen due to an announcement by the company or news speculation. Here, the investor could sell the share while it is at a peak, cash in on the gain, and then buy again at a lower price when the price comes down.
- Business Life Cycle – You realise the business' life cycle has passed its growth stage and peaked at its highest, so you prepare an exit strategy to sell all or offload some of your shares for a profit.

Ultimately, if you sell your shares and have made a profit you can safely regard this as a good decision.

However, if you sell your shares and make a loss, it could also be a good decision. For example, Share A has been underperforming and you have sold it and incurred a loss. From these proceeds of the sale, you have invested into Share B which is now performing better and so now you are on the road to recover the loss you made previously. Therefore, it was a good decision to sell share A.

Property Investment vs Share Investment

Let's analyse and assess the pros and cons of property investment versus share investment.

Property Investment

Generally, many consider property to be a safer investment and is mostly regarded as a long-term investment.

Pros

- Creates equity in your residential home for a period of time.
- Allows you to have a greater borrowing power to obtain further loans to build a portfolio.
- Property can act as security for future investment properties.
- Investment properties generate passive income over a period of time.
- Governments provide incentives to purchase residential homes such as concession on stamp duty and the first home buyers grant.
- To buy a property, you only need a 10%-20% deposit and the rest can be paid over a period of time.
- Investment properties will generally give you a better return on investment.
- Property is a tangible asset.

Cons

- Involves a huge outlay for the deposit.
- Could cause liquidity problems as you cannot sell immediately as there are various processes that must be followed before a property can be listed on the market.
- Requires ongoing maintenance depending on the age of the property.
- The property may be vacant for a period of time if the tenant vacates.
- Total rent generated may not cover the monthly mortgage and hence one would be out of pocket every month.
- When you buy a property, you will need legal representation.
- When an investor is buying and selling properties in the short-term, the overall capital gain would not be high as a result of the costs involved in buying and selling the property and the fact that most properties do not achieve high growth in a short period of time.

Share Investment

As shares do not require a substantial outlay in dollar value, an investor may have a variety of shares in their portfolio. Unlike property, shares may not be regarded as a long-term investment due to their volatility and quicker selling process. Investors may sell and cash in on the capital gain in a short period.

Pros

- Shares have a lower upfront cost.
- Shares are easier to transact when it comes to buying and selling.
- Shares are easy to liquidate and you can receive your money within a couple of days.
- You can buy or sell shares yourself and do not require legal representation.

Cons

- Investment in shares is riskier due to their volatility and can lead to financial ruin if not carefully planned.
- Unlike property investment, you cannot obtain a loan from the bank based on your current portfolio.
- You will not have an equity or redraw facility to use for future investments.
- Shares are not tangible assets.

PART 6 – ECONOMIC INSIGHT

16. BRIEF ECONOMIC INSIGHT

It is an added advantage to have a sound understanding of how the economy affects your investments.

In reference to the housing market, when the demand for housing is high and supply is low, you will often see property prices rise. Subsequently, when the supply is high but demand is low, the house prices tend to fall.

There are other factors associated with movement in the economy such as interest rate, inflation, GDP, employment, etc.

I will touch base on two main aspects which are interest rate and inflation.

Interest Rate

In Australia, the official interest rate is determined by the Reserve Bank of Australia and is assessed at the beginning of each month (except in January). The Reserve Bank reviews the economy to determine whether to increase, decrease, or hold the official cash rate, which may be based on the current economic and global outlook and inflation.

The movement of the interest rate will have an impact on investments and on the financial markets.

Increase in interest rate:

- Increase in mortgage repayments
- Less spending
- Dollar value tends to strengthen
- Investment yield on bonds will be increased
- Future investments tend to decline

Reduction in interest rate:

- Decrease in mortgage repayments
- More spending
- Dollar value tends to weaken
- Investment yield on bonds will be reduced

- Will lead to new investments, such as in property and shares

Inflation

In simple terms, inflation can be defined as the rising price of goods and services within an economy. Inflation is part of the Reserve Bank of Australia's monetary policy and the target is to maintain it within the vicinity of 2 - 3%. The current inflation in Australia is 6.1%, as reportec in July 2022.

Inflation is monitored through the consumer price index (CPI). CPI is a measure of the cost of a basket of goods and services bought by household consumers.

High inflation will reduce the power of money to purchase goods. If the prices of goods and services increase, it becomes less affordable to purchase goods and services at the current point in time.

During the rise of inflation, the prices of goods and services rise steeply and lead to consumers seeking a wage increase in order to compensate for the increased inflation rate.

When inflation is low, spending is low, which may lend a sense of uncertainty to the economy. In a period of low inflation, consumers' confidence erodes. Consumers tend to save during this time instead of spending which could further decrease economic growth.

Inflation plays an important role in the Reserve Bank's decision-making to determine whether the cash rate is to be increased or reduced. The movement in the interest rate is designed to either stimulate the economy to encourage spending or to slow down the economy to reduce spending.

Low inflation rate: the Reserve Bank may reduce the cash rate to stimulate the economy. Once the interest rate is reduced you would be paying less interest per month on your loan and have additional cash to spend. With low interest rates, people can borrow more but the downside is that people who have funds in their regular savings account will earn less interest.

High inflation rate: the Reserve Bank may increase the cash rate to slow down the economy. Once the interest rate is higher you would be paying more interest per month on your loan, have less cash to spend and would tend to borrow less. The upside is that people who have funds in their regular savings account will now earn more interest.

Low interest rates encourage spending, which leads to high inflation and when the interest rate has peaked, inflation will be slowed by the discouragement of spending.

Investors who rely on interest rate movements should not always take drastic actions based on economic predictions, particularly when interest rates will always rise and fall over time.

For instance, no one anticipated the Covid-19 pandemic followed by the war in Ukraine and Russia, which have both significantly affected the economy. When Covid hit Australia, there was huge panic in the markets. The Reserve Bank of Australia brought down the cash interest rate to the lowest level since its inception, at 0.10%, and inflation hovered around 2%.

While the cash rate was at its historic low level of 0.10%, the Reserve Bank announced that the rate would remain at this level until 2024. This announcement from the most respected financial body in Australia encapsulated the view that interest rates would not rise until 2024. However, the joy for lenders was short-lived for only 15 months until April 2022.

From May to September 2022, at the time of writing this book, there had been five interest rate rises bringing the cash rate to 2.35% and burdening property owners and investors, along with a current inflation rate of 6.1%.

The media reported banks predictions of what the interest rate will be by the end of December 2022 or by the first quarter of 2023, some having different predictions and even contradicting each other.

There is a lot to learn from this evaluation of the current economic situation and cash rate rises. We cannot take for granted what the economists predict.

When interest rates were at an all-time low, house prices were pushed significantly higher despite the country going through a pandemic. By then there was a speculation that there was a need for a rate rise.

Some banks had already started increasing the fixed rate from October 2021. For example, in October 2021, one of the four major banks was offering 2.49% fixed for two years and 2.59% fixed for three years.

In the June quarter of 2021, inflation was 3.8% and there was an indication that inflation was in a rising mode and monetary policy would follow its course to act.

In March 2022, the inflation rate increased to 5.1% and then to 6.1% in the June 2022 quarter. The RBA concurrently made four rate increases of 0.50% each month between June 22 and September 22.

When unexpected things happen, there may be no firm and ultimate answer for the investor. In that situation, there are things to look for as a guide. These simple guidelines may help save economic pain and burden for yourself and your family:

- Monitoring the inflation figure. If inflation tends to rise, there is a chance of an interest rate rise.
- Continuous increases in housing prices beyond affordability may also trigger an interest rate rise.
- Monitor the banks' fixed rate increases. The banks may start to increase the fixed home loan rate in anticipation of future cash rate rises by the Reserve Bank.
- Sudden increase in the price of goods will trigger high inflation.

These four factors may indicate the prospects of a future rate rise that might encourage investors to contemplate fixing their home or investment loan rate. If you're not sure, there are also options for having it both ways - partially fixed and partially variable interest rates.

Key Takeaway

Finally, to summarise, this book aims to give you a good understanding of what is entailed in investing and a guide to available investment strategies. It is an educational piece on how to invest wisely and lays out the pros and cons of certain investment techniques that will help you manage risk and avoid financial pitfalls.

It is not a get rich quick scheme, it is about generating a passive income for future retirement alongside your super or how to have enough investment earnings to substitute your current employment for early retirement.

The book includes the ingredients for how to invest and what to look for when you are planning to invest. It's about taking control of your investments and not totally relying on other people to make decisions for you. Yes, you may seek relevant advice but, at the end of the day, it is you who will make the ultimate call to invest.

As an investor, it is always advisable to take a hands-on approach and be in touch with the current economic climate and other contributing factors so that you can monitor the health of all your investments, whether they be in properties, term deposits or the stock market.

Made in the USA
Monee, IL
04 November 2026

67381718R00105